The Christian World Mission in Our Day

The Christian World Mission in Our Day

KENNETH SCOTT LATOURETTE

Sterling Professor of Missions and Oriental History, Emeritus,
and Associate Fellow of Berkeley College in Yale University

 Harper & Brothers Publishers New York

Library of Congress catalog card number: 54-5852

Contents

5

Preface

WHAT is the Gospel doing in our day? What is happening to the Church which it has brought into being and of which it is the vehicle? To what extent can we modify the developments? If we can modify them, in what direction should we move?

We are living in a world of change. That is one of the commonplaces of our time. Indeed, it is so much a commonplace that it is almost a banality. Therein lies a danger. In accepting it we are exposed to two perils. On the one hand, taking it as a matter of course, we do not seek to understand it or to search for its significance. On the other hand, submitting to it as inevitable, we have an attitude before it of resigned helplessness. If we succumb to either we do nothing about it and instead of moulding, even to some slight degree, the age into which we are being hurried, we permit ourselves to be moulded by it and by those who are striving to shape it. We become conformed to this world instead of being transformed and proving what is that good and acceptable and perfect will of God.

We live in one of the great days of the Church. Thanks to the inherent power of the Gospel and the labours of our predecessors, the Church is now represented in almost every land and among nearly every tribe and people. Of the countries which claim political independence, only three are without the organized, visible Church—Afghanistan, Nepal, and Outer

Mongolia. In many lands the Church is represented only by minorities, some of them feeble. In others it has drawn into its fellowship a substantial proportion of the population. Moreover, in new ways and quite rapidly, Christians are being drawn into a world-wide fellowship which transcends denominational and national barriers. That fellowship is by no means complete, but it is gaining in momentum. In our generation, for the first time in history, the Church can be called global.

Yet in this world of rapid change the Gospel is also confronted by powerful enemies. Some of them are old. Some are relatively new. Others are quite new. We who bear the Christian name are occasionally—or more than occasionally—tempted to focus our attention upon the enemies and think of the Church as on the defensive. We note numerical losses in parts of what we have been accustomed to regard as Christendom and listen despondently to those who tell us that we are living in the early stages of the post-Christian era. We forget that this is not the picture which Christ gave of the Church. In one of the two places in which the record quotes him as using the word "Church" he speaks of evil as on the defensive, a besieged city, with gates which are not to be able to resist the Church. The imagery seems to be that of a siege, perhaps prolonged, rather than of quick and successful assault, but Christ was confident of victory. When and precisely how it would come he did not say, but he had no doubt of the outcome. In the nineteen centuries of its existence, brief when compared with the total sweep of human history, the Church has known times of retreat as well as advance, but the total course thus far has been forward.

Whether the record of the years immediately ahead will be

ones of gain rather than loss depends in part upon us who now make up the "Church militant." We cannot be privy to all the counsels of God. We are assured that God's word is not to return to Him void but is to accomplish what He pleases. Yet His thoughts, so we are told, are not our thoughts, neither are our ways His ways. But we are also told that we are co-labourers with God, privileged by Him to share in His work. If we prove faithless to that trust there may be delay, with unimaginable suffering and loss to many of our contemporaries. If we are faithful we can confidently leave the outcome with God.

If we are to be faithful we must seek to understand the situation in which we find ourselves and to devise and carry through ways of meeting it. It is that which is the reason for the pages which follow.

First of all we must try to see the main features of the age which is now yesterday, the one immediately preceding that into which we have been ushered, and the manner in which the Gospel was brought to bear upon the world of that day. In the main the record of those who then sought to proclaim the Gospel, to make disciples of the nations, and to teach them to observe all that Christ commanded was noble and notable. In their endeavour they developed methods and institutions which we have inherited, but which are not necessarily fitted to the conditions which are now upon us.

We must next go on to describe the main features of our day, pointing out the contrasts with yesterday, the major forces which are operating, their bearing upon the Gospel, and the achievements of the world mission thus far in our age. So far the task is one of analysis. It is challenging but not impossible. In all this, both yesterday and in our day, we must seek to

9

understand how God works. We must do so that we may know better how to work with Him. This requires us to ask what the Gospel is and to inquire how it operates in history. As we strive to discern the way in which God works we must ask afresh the nature of the missionary obligation of the Church.

There follows what is more difficult, the framing of feasible and wise procedures for the years immediately ahead, procedures which shall be in accord with God's thoughts and ways. Here especially we must disclaim infallibility. Nor can we afford to be inflexible. The world in which we live is extraordinarily fluid. The main forces are fairly obvious, but the combinations which they will assume are unpredictable. We must be prepared for quick shifts in our programs. We must not sit idle but must venture forth courageously, hopefully, and in faith. Our main purpose has been defined for us by our Lord and the nature of the Gospel. The application has been entrusted to us by God. God has promised His presence and the guidance of His Holy Spirit, but He does not dictate to us. He does not wish automata but sons in His service. He recognizes our frailty and our proneness to mistakes, but He asks us to use to the full such knowledge and powers of reason as He has given us, even though we will from time to time be in error.

The challenge is urgent and brooks no delay. Great forces are operating. The chief enemies are pervasive and resourceful. We must both plan and act.

As we plan and act we also do well to look toward the culmination. What, so far as we can discern it, is to be the end of it all? What is to be the harvest? What is to be the consummation of history?

From the above outline it is quite clear that by the Christian world mission we mean just that. We must view the entire world and not merely one segment of it. God so loved the world, not just a portion of it, and He sent His son into the world that the world might be saved through him. Our Lord taught us to pray, "Thy kingdom come, Thy will be done on earth as it is in heaven." God's kingdom is without territorial or other boundaries. This, indeed, is one of the lessons which God seems to be seeking to teach us in our day. Whatever the time or the manner of the consummation of God's plan, it embraces the whole creation. God's purpose, we are told, is to gather together in one all things in Christ, both which are in heaven and which are on earth. The apostle assures us that the creation which has been groaning in travail was subjected to futility in hope, and that, waiting in eager longing for the revelation of the sons of God, it is ultimately to be set free from its bondage to decay and is to obtain the glorious liberty of the children of God.

In one or another form the substance of this little book has been given as the Layne Lectures at the New Orleans Baptist Theological Seminary, as a Henry Wright Lecture at the Yale University Divinity School, as the Smyth Lectures at the Columbia Theological Seminary, and as the Wilkinson Lectures in the Northern Baptist Theological Seminary, all in 1953, and as lectures under the auspices of the faculties of theology at the University of Lund, the University of Copenhagen, and the University of Helsinki, all in March, 1954. For the unfailing courtesy of these institutions the author is deeply grateful.

The book has, obviously, been written by a Christian and for Christians. It is to be hoped that some others than Christians may also find it of interest and through it obtain something of the Christian outlook on the world and, therefore, a glimpse into what the Christian believes to be the true understanding of the world.

Those familiar with the author's other books will find in the following pages much that has a familiar sound. The author has consciously been repeating, although in summary and in other words, some of the analyses and convictions which he has expressed elsewhere. Even so, those who are thoroughly familiar with the author's earlier books will find this reiteration useful as a background to the main purposes of this book.

As in most of what he has written, the author is deeply indebted to Mrs. Charles T. Lincoln for her skilful typing and suggestions as to literary style.

The Christian World Mission in Our Day

CHAPTER I

The World of Yesterday

WHAT was the world of yesterday? When did it begin? When did it end? What were its chief characteristics?

The world of yesterday may be said to have been bounded by the years 1815 and 1914. These, as all students of history will recognize, are respectively the dates which mark the end of the Napoleonic Wars and the beginning of what we call World War I. Yet it is seldom that one age can be marked off from another so precisely. Periods in history have a way of beginning and ending gradually, of having their inception while the immediate predecessor is still dominant, and of surviving, although fading, after their successor has come to birth. So it is with that world of yesterday. Some of its most striking features began before 1815 and several are still with us, not a few of them in intensified form, nearly a generation after 1914.

In general, seven features mark off that yesterday from the days before it and the first four distinguish it from the day which has followed it. We will first name them and then say something about each, but, necessarily, in very summary fashion. (1) The era was one of comparative peace. (2) It was marked by a prodigious burst of creative energy, wealth, and power among Occidental peoples, with striking changes in their civilization. (3) In the main, for the Western world it was a time of optimism. (4) The century witnessed the rapid expansion of the Occident and the domination of most of the earth by it

15

and its culture. (5) That expansion brought about the beginnings of revolutions in the cultures of most of the rest of mankind. (6) All of this had its origin in the traditional Christendom and radiated from it. (7) In that Christendom a seeming paradox was seen. On the one hand were the most open large defections from the Christian faith which had occurred since the rise and early spread of Islam and on the other as great awakenings in what may be called Christianity as had ever been known.

(1) The century was one of comparative peace. In contrast with the preceding and the succeeding century no general European war engrossed the attention and wasted the energies of Christendom. Wars there were. Europe itself knew several, among them that bearing the name of Crimea, the Six Weeks' War (between Prussia and Austria), and the Franco-Prussian War, but compared with those in some of the preceding centuries they were all brief, involved only a few powers, and were not exhausting. In the United States the Civil War was more costly in lives and treasure than any of the conflicts in Europe, and in China the T'ai P'ing Rebellion may have taken an even greater toll in lives, but both were confined to one country and did not become general. There were also wars on the periphery of the expanding Europeans, such as those with the Indians in the United States, with the Maoris in New Zealand, with various states and elements in India, and the Boer War in South Africa. None of these, however, engaged more than a fraction of the Occidental peoples and all were purely local. There was no global conflict akin to those of the six decades before 1815 or in the generation which followed 1914. Plans were hopefully made for the elimination of all war.

(2) The comparative peace of the century facilitated a creative burst of energy in the Occident with a resulting phenomenal increase in manufactures, wealth, and population in that section of mankind. It was the era of the industrial revolution, of the rapid development of the natural sciences, and of mechanical inventions including new methods of transportation and communication (the steamship, the steam and electric railways, the automobile, the telegraph, the telephone, and the electric light). Factories multiplied and cities increased in numbers and size. Anesthetics and antiseptics made possible spectacular advances in surgery. Micro-organisms were discovered and the beginnings of safeguards against them were developed. Populations mounted. Wealth increased at a breath-taking rate with huge fortunes for the few and comfort for a substantial minority. Theories for the reorganization of society were formulated with the object of enabling more of mankind to share in the good things of life. Political democracy, given a great impulse by the American and French Revolutions of the preceding period, spread rapidly. Socialism in some of its many forms, notably that associated with the name of Marx, was elaborated, in protest against the prevailing *laissez-faire*. All this brought striking changes in the civilization of the Occident, changes which were to mount after 1914.

(3) Under these circumstances it is not surprising that optimism characterized the Occident. Pessimists were not lacking. Some of them were rebels who denounced the evils in the civilization about them. Some were painfully aware of the insecurity and the evils in Western civilization. Others temperamentally found it difficult to be hopeful. However, the general atmosphere made it easy to believe in progress. The theory of evolu-

17

tion, then first propounded, was so interpreted as to support a confidence that the course of mankind was onward and upward forever. Struggle was recognized, but it was regarded as the way through which a perfect age was ultimately to be achieved. That age was to come, so many believed, by a combination of human effort and the automatic, inevitable course of history.

(4) This burgeoning, prosperous Occident expanded until its peoples and their culture dominated the globe to a greater degree than had previously been true of any group of mankind. That expansion had begun late in the fifteenth century with the discovery by Europeans of America and the sea route around Africa to India and the Far East. It was now accelerated. European peoples poured into the Americas, especially the United States, and into Australia, New Zealand, and South Africa. From that vast migration new nations arose and some which were already incipient attained unprecedented dimensions. The new nation of predominantly European stock which had the largest growth was the United States. By 1914 in area, wealth, and population it had become one of the major powers of the earth. European countries built colonial empires. The chief of these were those of France, Russia, and Great Britain. The Russian Empire was territorially continuous, except for a few adjacent islands a solid block of territory across the northern stretches of Eurasia. The largest of the empires was that of Great Britain. The proud boast was made that on it the sun never set. It embraced large portions of the Americas, Australia, New Zealand, some of the islands in the Pacific, extensive sections of Africa, the vast sub-continent of India, the neighbouring Ceylon and Burma, and strategic stations on most of the major sea routes of the globe. Great Britain led the way in the industrial revo-

lution, its capital became the banking centre of the world, and its navy and its commercial fleets dominated the seas. By the year 1914 European peoples or peoples of European descent controlled most of the land surface of the globe. Such peoples as maintained their political independence of the Occident were adopting some of the features of Occidental culture. The features which they favoured were machines and other mechanical devices, science, engineering, and the forms of education by which these were transmitted and furthered.

(5) The expansion of European peoples and the impact of Occidental civilization began to work revolutions in the cultures of the peoples upon whom they impinged. Those revolutions were most marked and thoroughgoing in cultures which are usually termed "primitive." They were seen among the tribes of American Indians, most notably in the United States. By the year 1914 in some of the islands of the Pacific they had gone very far, especially in several of the smaller groups. By that year they had begun in Africa south of the Sahara. On the eve of 1914 elements committed to the revolution had seized control of Turkey and China. The resulting disintegration usually was most rapid among "primitive" folk, but it was beginning to be marked among the Chinese. By the year 1914 that most numerous of the fairly homogeneous groups of mankind and one possessed of an ancient high civilization was in the early stages of a revolution which after that year was to sweep it from its historic moorings and to have effects which were to be both startling and bewildering.

(6) One of the most thought-provoking features of the period between the years 1815 and 1914 was that these tremendous movements which were reshaping mankind had their rise

and most extensive development in Christendom, a region in which Christianity had long been potent, and among peoples and nations which were usually called Christian. In that hopeful age there were Christians who pointed to them as evidence of the beneficent effect of the Gospel. Here, however, was a problem which was by no means so simple. It was not certain that the Gospel was chiefly responsible for this burst of energy. That it was one of the causes was fairly clear. It could be shown to be a factor in the emergence of at least some of the major features of Western civilization of the nineteenth century. This was true of several of the prevailing social and political theories including democracy and at least some forms of socialism. The Gospel was obviously the major source of several of the efforts to correct the evils and abuses of the day. This could be proved, for instance, of the abolition of Negro slavery, prison reform, the origin of the Red Cross, and movements to curb war and promote peace among the nations. If the claim were made that the science and machines of the Occident were primarily the outgrowth of Greek thought, a plain fact stood stubbornly in the way. South and east of the Mediterranean was the Moslem world. It, too, was the heir of Greek culture. Indeed, some of the knowledge of that culture had come through it to Western Europe. Yet that knowledge had originally reached the Moslems through Christians and the promising beginnings of science in the Moslem-Arab world had languished as the Christian communities in its midst had dwindled. The most palpable difference between the cultures north and south of the Mediterranean was that the one had preserved the Christian heritage and the other had substituted for it Islam. Whether here was the major source of the achievements of Western European peo-

20

ples in the nineteenth century no one could either prove or disprove.

If here was the decisive cause, could the Gospel be held responsible for the evils which attended that burst of life in Western Europe? Could there be laid at its door, to mention only a few of the obvious blots on the nineteenth-century Occident, the festering slums of the industrial cities, the exploitation of the underprivileged and of the peoples upon whom the Occident impinged, the accentuation of crass materialism by the mounting wealth, and the horrors soon to be added to war? Here is a haunting question which is even more urgent in our day. We must face it again when we come to describe the present age. It may be that we shall find in it some clue to the fashion in which God acts in history through the Gospel.

(7) Closely associated with the perplexing fact of the reciprocally contradictory developments issuing from Christendom is that sobering paradox to which we have called attention. In "Christian" Europe, on the one hand, there was a more open departure from the Christian faith by large elements in the population than had been known since the great wave of Moslem conquest in the seventh and eighth centuries tore away about half of the then Christendom. On the other hand, there were striking revivals of the faith which, as we are to see in the next chapter, contributed to a more extensive spread of Christianity than it or any other religion had previously known.

The defections from Christianity were in part a continuation of what had been in progress since at least the Renaissance but which had become especially prominent in the eighteenth century. They were ostensibly largely on intellectual grounds, but were also in part against the Church as an institution. Many

had come to believe that Christianity was contrary to reason—
and that in spite of the fact that some, perhaps most of the first-
class minds in the Occident remained sincere believers. The
emphasis upon man's competence which came with the humanism of the Renaissance and also absorption in literature, art,
philosophy, or politics to the neglect of religion which characterized the Renaissance and its immediate aftermath did not at
first lead to an overt repudiation of Christianity. A nominal
connexion with the Church was maintained, even though with
criticism of some of its features. The eighteenth century emphasized reason and under that influence and the value placed on
what was called "free thought" Deism became fashionable.
Deism was by no means atheistic. It believed in God and in immortality, but it held that these were supported by reason and
many of its advocates scoffed at the distinctively central Christian conviction of the act of God in the Incarnation. Before the
century was out some thinkers, such as Hume, were challenging
the basic assumptions of those who depended upon reason, but
without returning to the Christian faith. The French Revolution had Deists among its leaders and during its more radical
stage sought to substitute Deism for Christianity.

In the nineteenth century in many quarters the rationalistic
approach continued. Open attacks on Christianity were made
—some on the Continent of Europe by such men as Nietzsche,
by a grim irony and perhaps significantly from a lineage of
Protestant pastors, some in England, and some in a more popular vein in America, notably by Robert Ingersoll, the son of a
Congregational minister. Less forthright but possibly more
destructive was much of the philosophy of the century. Some
conclusions of the historical study of the Bible undermined for

many confidence in the reliability of that book, so basic to Christian faith. To thousands the science of the nineteenth century seemed to make belief difficult or impossible. The theory of evolution, associated with the name of Darwin, and the findings of geology appeared to many to invalidate the account of the creation in the first chapters of Genesis. The rise of sociology and the study of the history of religion led numbers to view Christianity as one of many religions, like the others a purely human development, part of the growth of cultures and civilization. Characteristically the term "agnostic" was coined as descriptive of the position of those who regarded the evidence as insufficient to warrant either the rejection or the wholehearted acceptance of Christianity. Many believed the Church and its faith to stand in the way of progress. Thousands among the labourers in the factories regarded the Church as a bulwark of the classes which were exploiting them. Karl Marx was notably bitter in his denunciations. Others looked upon the Church, especially the Roman Catholic Church, as an obstacle to the political liberalism which they were promoting and endeavoured to reduce or entirely to abolish its power in the state and its control of education and marriage. Nominally the vast majority of the population in Europe maintained a formal standing in the Church. They were baptized, a large proportion were confirmed, and marriage in the Church and burial from it remained social conventions. However, in the movements of population across the seas, notably to the United States, the danger of dropping even such remnants of church ties was great. Moreover, in the shifts of population to the new industrial and mining centres thousands lost touch with the Church. This was not necessarily from hostility but rather from inertia and indifference. To multitudes religion, including the Christian religion, seemed to be one of the accessories of living, possibly useful, but not essential and quite dispensable. To many Christianity appeared to be a fading phenomenon of civilization. Yet this was only one side of the paradox.

In striking contrast with the apparent recession of the Christian tide there were great bursts of fresh life in the churches. These were seen in all three of the main branches of the Church —the Orthodox, the Roman Catholic, and the Protestant—but were especially marked in the last two and particularly in Protestantism.

The century witnessed the reëmergence of some of the Orthodox Churches as the Turkish tide waned. This was true in Greece, Bulgaria, Rumania, and Serbia. It also saw stirrings of life in the Russian Orthodox Church which brought about recovery from the low ebb in the eighteenth century.

The Roman Catholic Church had borne the main brunt of the scepticism of the eighteenth century and the French Revolution. It also suffered from the adverse currents of the nineteenth century. The wars of independence in Spanish America dealt severe blows to the Church in that largest body of Roman Catholics outside of Europe. The anti-clerical agitation and legislation in the Americas and Europe were chiefly directed against it. The de-Christianization which was under way among a large part of its constituency was more marked in France than in any other country in Europe. The Popes whose reigns covered most of the century appeared to hasten the defections. They were denunciatory of the movements which they deemed hostile to the faith, movements which seemed to gain in momentum as the century proceeded, such as the separation of

Church and state, the toleration of other faiths than Roman Catholicism, the control of education by the state and the attendant weakening of religious instruction in the schools, civil marriage, and, in Italy, the elimination of the Papal States. The Popes also strove to extirpate root and branch the "modernism" by which some of the best brains among the clergy and laity endeavoured to reconcile the historic faith of the Church with the intellectual currents which were sweeping across Europe. In several countries a large proportion of the property of the Church and its monasteries was confiscated and actions were taken to curtail the share of monastic orders and congregations —priests, nuns, and lay brothers—in the schools. The Jesuits were especially singled out for attack.

Yet the Roman Catholic Church had a striking renewal. The Society of Jesus, which had been dissolved late in the eighteenth century, was revived. Some of the monastic orders which had been adversely affected by the French Revolution and the Wars of Napoleon were restored. Many new monastic orders and societies of men and women came into being. Indeed, more of them arose in the nineteenth century than in any other one hundred years of the Church's history. Movements sprang up to enlist the activity of the rank and file of the laity. Among them were Catholic Action and the Knights of Columbus. Through the spread of the special devotion to the Sacred Heart of Jesus which had become prominent in the seventeenth century loyalty to Christ and his sacrifice on the Cross was cultivated. The formal proclamation of the Immaculate Conception of the Virgin Mary as a dogma of the Church enhanced the honour that had been traditionally paid to the Mother of Christ. Frequent communion by the laity was encouraged and spread.

25

The power of the Pope was strengthened. Theoretically this entailed no radical change. The Popes had long claimed to be the divinely authorized guardians of the Christian faith and to have full executive power over the entire Church. However, even within the Roman Catholic Church the administrative authority of the Popes had been effectively challenged by monarchs and by some of the bishops. In states which were staunchly orthodox in doctrine as it was expounded by the Papacy, such as Spain, and where the Inquisition was employed to eliminate heresy, the Papal claims to control the Church had been denied both in theory and in practice. In France, where the monarchs had protested their orthodoxy and where the mightiest of them, Louis XIV, had persecuted the Protestants, Gallicanism, namely, the autonomy of the Church in France as against the Pope, had been strong. In the nineteenth century what was known as Ultramontanism triumphed, namely, the power of the Pope over all the branches of the Roman Catholic Church.

The enhancement of the power of the Popes was due to a number of factors. The anti-clericalism which developed in most countries that had been known as Catholic, anti-clericalism which in some led to the full disestablishment of the Church, tended to lead the bishops and clergy to seek the support of the Popes and to put themselves under their direction. This was facilitated by the historic Papal claims. The improvement of transportation and communication through the peace and the mechanical devices of the century shortened the time distances to Rome and made easy travel to that city and direction from it.

The augmented power of the Popes was seen in a number of ways. The Popes controlled more effectively the appointment of bishops throughout the Church and supervised the bishops and

THE WORLD OF YESTERDAY

the clergy more closely than before. Through central bureaus in Rome they kept in touch with and directed more minutely than at any earlier time the various activities of the many organizations on all the widely flung frontiers of the Church. By taking the initiative in proclaiming as dogma the Immaculate Conception and by having that decree accepted without serious protest, the Pope strengthened the precedent for his power to define the doctrine of the Church. That power was spectacularly confirmed by the action of the Vatican Council in 1870 in endorsing Papal infallibility in matters of faith and morals. In the latter part of the century, moreover, the Papal throne was fortunate in having as occupants first Leo XIII who by a combination of tact and firmness greatly enhanced the respect shown his office throughout much of the world, and next his successor, Pius X, of such undeniable sanctity that in the mid-twentieth century he was formally declared to be blessed, presumably a first step toward canonization.

In consequence of these several developments, by 1914 more than at any previous time the Roman Catholic Church tended to be a closely knit body under one directing head and supported by a loyal army of clergy, religious orders, and laity. Although in some countries still ostensibly the church of the overwhelming majority, increasingly it was a minority set in a consciously hostile world. Yet it was not primarily on the defensive, but was reaching out to win that world to its faith.

Even more than the Roman Catholic Church, in the nineteenth century the Protestant forms of the faith were tremendously strengthened by revivals and spread until they were represented by churches in most of the peoples and countries of the world. This was the more remarkable in view of the seeming weakness of Protestantism at the outset of the century through its many divisions and the subservience to the state of the churches to which the large majority of its adherents belonged, and because, in contrast with the Roman Catholic Church, which was already present in all of the larger and many of the smaller countries of the world, Protestantism was to be found only in a small segment of the globe.

May we pause for a moment to amplify this last sentence. In the year 1815 Protestantism had no unity except in its common heritage in the Gospel, in its dissent from the Roman Catholic Church, and in distinctive principles held in common, namely, salvation by faith alone and its corollaries, the priesthood of all believers and the right and duty of the individual Christian to judge for himself in questions of belief. At the very outset of the Protestant movement these principles were strikingly manifested in Luther, never more vividly than when in the presence of the assembled representatives of Church and state he stood staunchly for what he had found true through his own personal experience, refusing to submit to their judgement unless he was convinced through Scripture and what appealed to him as sound reason. Only a few small bodies carried these principles to their logical conclusion. The varying extent to which they were implemented by different churches brought division. Still more, the principles themselves, even when imperfectly followed, made for seemingly endless fissiparousness. By its nature, as Roman Catholics hopefully declared, Protestantism appeared doomed to end in a weak welter of confusion. Within particular political units, Protestantism was given a degree of uniformity by the state. In each of the many principalities and kingdoms which composed the Germany of 1815 the ruler controlled the Church, if it was Protestant, and strove, with fair success, to prevent dissent. That was also true in the Scandinavian kingdoms. In England, Wales, and Ireland there was an established church, but King and Parliament had been unable to prevent dissent and had been constrained, reluctantly, to come to terms with it. Even here nonconformity was under discouraging disabilities. However, subordination to the state might well curb and perhaps stifle the inner life of the churches. In 1815, Protestantism, apparently thus weakened and handicapped, was almost entirely regional, a phenomenon of the British Isles and the north-western corner of the continent of Europe. So far as it had any religion, the United States was prevailingly Protestant, but less than a tenth of its population were members of churches and the nation was young and as yet only sparsely settled. Small Protestant communities were to be found in British North America, the West Indies, Dutch and British Guiana, South Africa, Ceylon, India, and the East Indies, but together they totalled less than a million. The neutral observer might have been pardoned if he had appraised Protestantism as a passing phase of Christianity which by its very nature was fatally weak and had largely spent its force.

Yet within this seemingly unpromising wing of Christianity vitality was already making itself felt in fresh, vigorous movements. Although thus far affecting only minorities, they were soon to swell to major proportions. Under their impulse and through them, by 1914 Protestants had carried their faith to almost all countries and peoples and had begun to reach out in quite new ways to an inclusive unity. After 1914, as we are to see, both this geographic expansion and this movement toward unity continued.

29

The awakening in Protestantism which worked these spectacular results was seen first in Germany late in the seventeenth century where it gave rise to Pietism and shaped the Moravians. True to the Protestant genius, it made much of a direct, personal experience of salvation. By 1815 the Pietist movement had taken root in Scandinavia. From it began to issue missions to non-Christians, chiefly from Halle and the Moravians at Herrnhut, but as yet on only a small scale. In the first half of the eighteenth century there broke out almost simultaneously in England and the Thirteen Colonies which later became the United States what were known respectively as the Evangelical Awakening and the Great Awakening. The Evangelical Awakening was associated with the Wesleys, through them was indebted to the Moravians, and had as one of its outgrowths the Methodism which in the nineteenth century was to become world-wide. Yet it was not confined to Methodism but affected other religious bodies in England, both the Church of England, in which a strong Evangelical wing arose, and the several nonconforming Protestant denominations. The Great Awakening had as its most notable leader the intellectually brilliant, morally earnest, and vividly mystical Jonathan Edwards. It both reinforced and was reinforced by the Evangelical Awakening. During the storm of the war by which the Thirteen Colonies achieved their independence, the Great Awakening died down. However, it surged forth afresh in the 1790's in New England in what is sometimes called the Second Great Awakening. Moreover, late in the eighteenth century and in the first few years after 1800 revivals broke out elsewhere in the United States, notably through camp-meetings on the western frontier. After 1815 these revivals or awakenings in Protestantism mounted. They made themselves felt throughout that wing of the faith. Pietism continued in the various Lutheran churches on the Continent of Europe and had many expressions, both in Germany and in Scandinavia. The revivals also stirred the Reformed Churches on the Continent, whether in Germany, Switzerland, France, or the Netherlands. They were especially potent in the United States, the British Isles, and the rapidly growing British colonies. In the United States the outstanding leaders were Charles G. Finney in the fore part and Dwight L. Moody in the latter half of the century. Both Finney and Moody preached extensively in Britain as well as in the United States. Thanks to the revivals, the Protestant churches in the United States grew by leaps and bounds, the nonconforming churches in England, Wales, and Ireland were greatly strengthened in numbers and vigour, the Presbyterianism of Scotland was revitalized, and the Evangelical wing of the Church of England became prominent.

The revivals in Protestantism had much in common and their expressions, while varied, had a family likeness. True to the Gospel and the Protestant genius, they all stressed a personal commitment in faith, individual conversion, and the cultivation of the life of the spirit through Bible study, prayer, public worship, and preaching. They also gave rise to many efforts to combat the clamant ills of mankind. From them came the movements which abolished the African slave trade and Negro slavery in the British Empire and the United States. They contributed to prison reform, to better care of the insane and the feeble-minded, to the rise of the modern nursing profession, to legislation to shorten the hours of labour and, especially in the British Isles, in other ways to improve the living and working conditions of those employed in the factories and mines which were accompaniments of the industrial revolution. They stimulated improved education for the masses. They were the direct source of the Red Cross for the alleviation of the suffering arising from wars and natural disasters. They spurred many to work for peaceful ways for the adjustment of disputes among nations. They were the chief inspiration to attempts to curb the degrading use of alcoholic beverages. They gave rise to fresh organizations and denominations. From them sprang the Young Men's Christian Associations to serve the white collar class in the great cities and the Salvation Army to bring individual salvation and physical ministry to the denizens of the slums. From them issued such new denominations as the Plymouth Brethren in the British Isles and the Disciples of Christ and the Christian Churches in the United States.

The revivals contributed to the growing liberty of conscience and the progressive freeing of the Protestant churches from the control of governments which were among the prominent aspects of the religious history of the nineteenth century. Progress in these directions was seen on the Continent of Europe, but it was more marked in the British Isles and was especially characteristic of the United States and the new nations which arose from white settlement within the British Empire. The revivals were not the only cause. The growth of a multiplicity of denominations led the ones which were not espoused by the state to protest successfully against the preference shown to the established churches. But there were many who out of conviction insisted that if it were to be true to its divine commission the Church must be emancipated from control by the state.

The revivals brought a sense of unity to all who were committed to them, a unity which overpassed denominational barriers. The term "Evangelical" was adopted as descriptive of those who were stirred by the awakenings. Derived from the Greek word translated into English as "Gospel," the word "Evangelical" could be claimed by all who believed themselves true to the "Good News" in Christ. Indeed, it was employed by Roman Catholics and was a special favorite of Lutherans, whether or not they were Pietists. However, those stirred by the revivals, finding a kinship among all with a similar experience, regardless of denomination, believed that they saw in it a designation of their common faith. Increasingly they found that they were agreed on what to them were the outstanding and essential features of the Gospel and that, in general, they could concur in a formal statement of their basic convictions. Even before 1815 they had begun to coöperate in such bodies as the London Missionary Society, the American Board of Commissioners for Foreign Missions, and the Bible societies on both sides of the Atlantic. Between 1815 and 1914 the sense of community deepened and found increasing expression in organizations. Most of these organizations were composed of individuals and not of ecclesiastical bodies. Such were the Young Men's and the Young Women's Christian Associations, the Evangelical Alliance, the several student Christian movements which in 1895 joined in the World's Student Christian Federation, and the various bodies for the promotion of Sunday Schools which in 1907 organized the World's Sunday School Association. Here and there ecclesiastical bodies were devising ways of coöperation. Thus in 1908 the Federal Council of the Churches of Christ in America was constituted. Missionary societies, some of them officially controlled and supported by their respective churches, more and more worked together and in 1910 held the remarkable World Missionary Conference at Edinburgh. Here were the beginnings of what after 1914 came generally to be known as the Ecumenical Movement and which was to have an even greater growth after that year.

As might have been expected, and quite significantly, the movement toward unity among Protestants was strongest on the newest geographic frontiers of the faith. Coöperation went very far among missionaries in such countries as India, China, and Japan, where Protestantism was a relatively recent arrival and where numbers of denominations were represented in the missionary body. It also grew rapidly in the United States, where ecclesiastical differences were less firmly entrenched than in Europe, and where, living side by side on the basis of legal equality, denominations found that what they had in common in their faith was greater than what divided them. Increasingly, they learned from one another in methods and forms of worship, used one another's hymns, and found it to the advantage of the common Christian cause to work together.

The Protestant movement toward unity was beginning to attract more than those who, in the sense in which we have noted them as utilizing that designation, called themselves Evangelicals. In the first half of the nineteenth century a revival in the Church of England, often called the Oxford Movement, stressed the Catholic element which had been present in that Church from its beginning. It emphasized that which the Church of England had inherited from the Catholic Church of the early centuries before the many dissensions had rent it apart. Often designated as Anglo-Catholics, they were made unhappy by the Protestant elements in the Church of England.

Obviously it would not be easy for them to coöperate with those who were frankly Protestant. Yet some Anglo-Catholics were present at the World Missionary Conference at Edinburgh in 1910 and they were to have an increasing share in the Ecumenical Movement.

In this world of yesterday, between the significant years 1815 and 1914, Christianity had a growing and important place. The "Christian" peoples of the world, centring in Western Europe, were experiencing a phenomenal growth in numbers, wealth, and physical might. Their civilization was being re-shaped by powerful forces. They were expanding rapidly and they and their culture were dominating the world. Under their impact the cultures of the rest of mankind were in the early stages of profound revolution. To many observers it looked as though the words "Christian" and "Christendom" as applied to European peoples had become an anachronism. Adverse forces seemed to be too great for the hold which that faith had gained in earlier centuries. De-Christianization appeared to have set in. It seemed as though whatever of the Gospel had been accepted was being abandoned. Since Europe was the centre of "Christendom" and since there the Gospel had its chief hold, ground could be found for believing that Christianity was waning. Yet, by a strange paradox Christianity was displaying as great a revival as it had ever known. In that paradox may be had insights into the Gospel and the manner in which it works in the lives of men. To these insights we must return later. We must next, however, as a preliminary to attempts at still further understanding, note the spread of Christianity in the nineteenth century.

CHAPTER II

The Spread of the Gospel
in the World of Yesterday

IN that yesterday, the nineteenth century, the Gospel had a more extensive geographic spread than ever before. It also had a wider effect upon mankind as a whole than in any previous era.

As must be apparent from what has been said in the preceding chapter, this was in connexion with the expansion of European peoples and the penetration and domination of the planet by them and their culture. Presumably without this expansion that spread of Christianity would not have been. It is, therefore, tempting to regard it, as has often been done, as a phase and tool of Occidental imperialism, one of the agencies deliberately utilized to achieve mastery over the earth and its inhabitants for the gratification of the lust for wealth and power of the peoples of European stock.

However, the picture is by no means so simple. To see it and interpret it in that fashion is to miss some of its most salient features and to fail to understand it. It is true that in this expansion of the Occident there was much of selfishness, with heartless and even malicious exploitation. Thirst for adventure, pride of race and culture, eagerness for riches, ambition to leave to posterity the fame of a conqueror and empire-builder, urgent desire for raw materials and markets for the expanding manufactures

36

of the West, all entered. But there were many in commercial
and government circles who wished the impact and rule of the
Occident to benefit the peoples upon whom they impinged. To
be sure, in assuming "the white man's burden" many did so
with an air of patronizing and sincerely convinced superiority.
They believed that certain races, which included their own,
were born to rule and others to be ruled. Yet some took the
responsibilities of empire with humility and served with integrity and selfless devotion. For much of this last, especially among
the British, the major imperial power, the Gospel and the revivals in Christianity during the century were mainly responsible.

Moreover, the missionaries through whom the spread of
Christianity was largely accomplished to some degree sought to
divorce themselves from the political and economic ambitions
of their fellow-countrymen. It is true that most of them were
willing to accept and some even sought the protection of their
governments. They rejoiced in being able to obtain in the
treaties of the Western powers with China the inclusion of toleration for their activities and their converts. On occasion in more
than one country they appealed to the diplomatic and military
representatives of their respective governments for protection of
their treaty rights. In many lands they sought and accepted from
the ruling power financial subsidies for their schools. This was
seen among Russian Orthodox, Roman Catholics, and Protestants. For a time in the United States most of the federal offi-
cials who supervised government aid to the Indians were missionaries. However, missionaries had less support from governments than in any age since, early in the fourth century, Con-
stantine had espoused the Christian cause. Some, for conscience'
sake, refused to ask or accept indemnities for property destroyed

or lives lost. Many freely criticized acts of exploitation by their governments and by Westerners engaged in industry, mining, and commerce. Usually, indeed, coolness and even antagonism existed between missionaries and their non-missionary fellow-countrymen in business and government. Missionaries sought to take advantage of the access to non-Christians obtained through the commerce and empire-building of the Occident but they strove to make the impact of the Occident a blessing and not a curse.

In country after country and among people after people, missionaries, especially Protestant missionaries, were pioneers in introducing aspects of Western civilization which they believed would be of use to non-Europeans. They reduced scores of languages to writing. They initiated schools of Western types to give the kind of education which they foresaw would be needed in the world into which the people whom they served were being hurried. They made these schools available for girls as well as boys. They laid the foundations for medical and nursing professions utilizing skills developed in the Occident. They showed how public health could be promoted. They gave demonstrations, often the first, of what could be achieved in augmenting food supply by techniques, food plants, and methods of animal husbandry which had proved valuable in the West. All of this missionaries sought to do in a Christian context. By that is meant that they wished to bring in these features of Occidental civilization in such a way that those who took them over would do so in the spirit of unselfish service and as displaying the radiance of the Gospel. In carrying out this purpose, missionaries often brought into existence continuing institutions. Among them were colleges, universities, hospitals, medical schools, nursing schools, demonstration farms, and rural coöperatives. These became one of the outstanding features of the missions of that yesterday and present one of the major problems to missions in the day that has followed.

These methods and institutions by no means constituted the whole of the multiform channels through which the missions of that yesterday sought to express and convey the Gospel. Russian Orthodox and Roman Catholic missions placed their chief emphasis upon planting the Church and strengthening it. Their aim was the salvation of souls for eternal life and to them the Church was the divinely appointed means to that end. The large majority of Protestant missionaries also had as their purpose bringing the wonder of the Gospel to as many as possible. However, they varied in their conviction as to how this could best be done. Most of them wished to aid in planting and nourishing churches. Early in the century some of those leading in Protestant missions declared that the purpose of the enterprise was to bring into being self-supporting, self-governing, and self-propagating churches. This remained the ostensible purpose of most of the societies through which Protestants carried on missions. Many missionaries, however, believed it to be their primary obligation to proclaim the Gospel to all men. They stressed the forms of the Great Commission which read: "Ye shall be my witnesses" and "Preach the Gospel to every creature." Remembering the promise, "This Gospel of the kingdom shall be preached in all the world for a witness unto all nations; and then shall the end come," they sought to hasten the consummation of the age by fulfilling what they believed to be its prerequisite. They were not primarily concerned to gather into churches those who believed. Some missionaries who gave themselves to institutions, such as schools and hospitals, hoped that through them the cultures about them would be leavened by the Gospel, but not necessarily through the conversion of individuals. This attitude was especially widespread in Moslem lands where direct conversions were almost impossible. In India and Moslem lands many missionaries who devoted their efforts to schools regarded them as a preparation for the Gospel, removing prejudice and producing character which, although not avowedly Christian, would have Christian features. As we have said, however, the majority of Protestant missionaries had as a major objective the emergence of churches which in time would bear the main responsibility for witnessing to the Gospel in their respective peoples, teaching them to observe all that Christ had commanded, and thus permeating and transforming cultures.

A striking feature of the missions of yesterday was the degree to which they enlisted the support of the rank and file of church members. Earlier missions had not been supported by the ordinary Christian. Orthodox and Roman Catholic missions had been carried on by monks, sometimes with the assistance of governments, but the average communicant had not regarded them as his concern. The early Protestant missions had been chiefly by special groups. The Moravians were an exception, for under the inspiration of their first great leader, Zinzendorf, they considered their entire church a missionary society. Now, in the nineteenth century societies were organized which sought to enlist all the laity in the support of missions by prayer and the giving of money. The earliest of these and the majority of them were among Protestants, but at least one was formed in the Russian Orthodox Church and there were several among Roman Catholics. Among Protestants on the Continent of

Europe and to a certain extent in the British Isles these societies were not officially espoused by the churches but gathered constituencies from among the churches. In the United States, however, increasingly the societies were sponsored by their respective denominations and the entire church was declared to be a missionary society. In spite of this expressed principle, in the United States as elsewhere, missions engaged the interest of only minorities, but those minorities were larger than ever before and grew as the century wore on. They are still growing.

Among Protestants missions became a concern of Christian students. The first large society in the United States, the American Board of Commissioners for Foreign Missions, was organized through the initiative of students in Andover Theological Seminary. Well along in the century, in 1886, the Student Volunteer Movement for Foreign Missions was born in a conference held under the direction of Dwight L. Moody. It swept through the colleges, universities, and theological seminaries of the United States and spread to the British Isles and Dominions and to the Continent of Europe. Through it and similar movements which it inspired, in the latter part of the nineteenth century thousands of students were recruited and went abroad under the missionary societies of their respective churches. There were few campuses on which more than a small minority were enlisted or were even deeply concerned, but in the aggregate those minorities were significant. The quadrennial conventions of the Student Volunteer Movement drew students from more institutions of higher learning in the United States and Canada than any other gatherings for any purpose, secular or religious.

The achievements through this missionary enterprise of yesterday were impressive. They were world-wide. In the traditional Christendom, Europe, they were much greater than is usually realized, even by those whose occupation it is to study the history of the Church. Although that body showed a renewed vigour, they were not particularly marked in the Russian Orthodox Church. Nor did that church have many missions among non-Christians outside of the Russian Empire. The one notable exception was in Japan, and here the Christian community which arose was not as large as those gathered by either Protestants or Roman Catholics. However, the Russian Orthodox Church had numbers of missions among non-Christians within the vast reaches of the Empire. Moreover, the nineteenth century witnessed the growth of Protestant bodies in Russia, especially those known as Evangelicals and Baptists. On the Continent of Europe, while losing multitudes, the Roman Catholic Church retained the loyalty of thousands of labourers in the multiplying factories and growing industrial cities. For the first time since the Protestant Reformation it gained footholds and toleration in Scandinavia. It also reëstablished its hierarchy in Great Britain and enjoyed a rapid growth on that island. This was chiefly through immigration from its constituencies in Ireland, but to some extent it was also through conversions.

On the Continent of Europe Protestantism was very active. In Germany what was known as the Inner Mission came into being. It sought to hold the masses who were drifting away from the faith and undertook various social services. Similar movements sprang up in Scandinavia. In France the McCall Mission endeavoured to reach the de-Christianized in the cities.

In Great Britain the achievements were particularly striking. Both the state and the free churches erected hundreds of new church buildings to care for the multiplying population and the growing urban areas. In Scotland the Free Church broke away from the Church of Scotland over the issue of control by secular interests and the state, thereby losing its share in the endowments and its physical equipment. But it built hundreds of church edifices and carried on foreign missions. The Church of Scotland, undiscouraged by the loss of a large and active element through the Free Church, also put up new church buildings in the growing cities. In Wales great revivals brought into the churches, especially the dissenting bodies, thousands who before had only nominal contacts with the Gospel. We have already noted the emergence of the Young Men's Christian Associations and the Salvation Army to reach important elements in the cities. Within the Church of England the Church Army, less prominent, arose somewhat on the pattern of the Salvation Army and for much the same purpose.

In the colonies which became the British Dominions of Canada, Australia, and New Zealand, the overwhelming majority of the immigrants were held to at least a professed allegiance to their inherited faith. This was in part through clergy and financial assistance from the British Isles, but it was chiefly through the initiative of the settlers themselves.

The major and most striking numerical successes of the Gospel in the nineteenth century were in the United States. In 1815 only a small minority of the white population, perhaps 10 per cent, held membership in any church. In addition there were the Indians, a still smaller minority of whom had been reached by the Gospel, and the rapidly growing Negro elements, most of them slaves, who were predominantly non-Christian. A vast westward movement of population was under way and

43

was to continue throughout the century, and there was danger that even such slight contact with the Gospel as most of the migrants had would be forgotten in the new environment. At the same time immigration was pouring in from Europe. In the Europe from which it came as a matter of long custom nearly all were baptized and had a formal connexion with the Church and to a large degree the Church was maintained by endowments or one form or another of taxation. In the United States the large majority were not baptized, there were very few ecclesiastical endowments, in only two or three states did any church have the benefit of public funds, and in them that aid was withdrawn before the first third of the century had passed. If church structures were to be built and clergy supported, it would have to be mainly out of the purses of the members. Moreover, cities grew rapidly and in them, as in Europe, conditions were adverse to the Gospel. In general the intellectual currents which in Europe were making it difficult for thousands to hold to their faith and were causing many to reject it were also sweeping across the United States. Numbers without a church connexion or who had divested themselves of one deliberately took that position, some ostensibly for intellectual reasons. For more inertia and lack of conviction were chiefly responsible. Under these circumstances there was grave danger that in the new nation which was coming into being such remnants of Christianity as survived would wane and disappear. As a matter of fact, just the opposite took place. The proportion of the population having church membership mounted fairly steadily and by 1914 was over two-fifths, or more than four times that of 1815.

This increase was due to success in meeting the several phases of the challenge. Gains were made on the westward moving frontier. While, in general, the percentage of church membership was progressively less the farther west one went, there was growth in all the main sections of the country. By 1914 about the same proportion of the Negroes and the Indians had membership in one or another of the churches as among the whites. A large proportion of the immigrants, those of Protestant, Roman Catholic, and Orthodox ancestry, were held to their hereditary faith and out of their poverty supported their clergy and built and maintained churches and parochial schools. In the cities the percentage of church membership seems to have been slightly higher than in the rural districts.

It was not merely in the percentage of church membership that the Gospel had an impact, apparently a growing impact, upon the United States. The word "apparently" is used because in other than the rather crude numerical realm accurate and even rough approximations at comparisons are difficult if not impossible. That is especially true of the degree to which members of churches exhibited the transforming power of the Gospel. That many were radiant examples of that power is certain, but most of them were humble folk who were not known or appreciated outside a small circle and there is no way of determining whether their number grew or, if it grew, how rapidly. Yet from the standpoint of the Gospel it is in this realm that the most important and significant fruits are to be seen. But it is clear that in many aspects of the life of the United States the Gospel was potent. That was seen in the abolition of Negro slavery, a movement which arose primarily from consciences made sensitive by the Gospel, in the many efforts, strikingly successful, of the white churches, especially in the field of education, to enable the

45

freedmen to adjust themselves to their new status, and particularly in the achievements of the Negro churches in furthering the advancement of members of their own race. It was not only in schools for Negroes that the Gospel contributed in the field of education. It was also in schools for other elements in the population. The majority of the colleges and universities and many of the secondary schools of the country owed their inception to Christian conviction and sacrifice. In more than one state it was a clergyman, moved by his faith, who stimulated the legislature to inaugurate universal primary education supported by public taxation. Better care for the insane, the temperance movement, the beginnings of higher education for women, and most of the private philanthropy which became one of the outstanding features of the United States were traceable to those who were inspired and sustained by the Gospel. The laws of the United States were profoundly influenced by Christian ideals.

So far as it was Christian the United States remained predominantly Protestant. Because of immigration the proportion of Roman Catholics increased, but in 1914 they were still a minority of all church members. Moreover, to the degree that Christianity had entered into the texture of the life of the nation it was mostly through Protestantism. The ideals of American democracy, with the value of the individual and the freedom and responsibility of the individual, came mainly from the extreme wing of Protestantism. It was both symbolic and significant that the most widely sung of the patriotic songs, expressing the aspirations of the nation, was *America* and that it was written by a Baptist clergyman.

In Latin America the nineteenth century proved difficult for the Roman Catholic Church. In 1815 it was the only form of

Christianity in the region. Indeed, both in that year and in 1914 here was the largest body of professed Roman Catholics outside of Europe. As we have suggested, the struggle for independence dealt severe blows to the Church, the more so because it was so dependent on Europe for its bishops and missionaries. After independence was gained, partial recovery was achieved, but this was largely through personnel from Europe: the Christianity of the area remained parasitic and of low grade. Moreover, anti-clericalism was chronic and anti-Christian currents from Europe, one of them Positivism, were potent, especially among the intelligentsia. However, Christianity in Latin America was strengthened by the entrance of other varieties of the faith. The Orthodox Churches gained a foothold through immigration. Protestantism flourished and began the growth which it continued even more strikingly after 1914. It entered partly through immigration, chiefly from Germany, through merchants, mainly from Great Britain, and particularly through missionaries. Some of the Protestant missionaries were from the British Isles, but most of them were from the United States. Thanks to these various factors, by 1914 Protestantism was represented in all the Latin American republics. It was especially strong in the largest of them, Brazil, and in Mexico.

Thus far we have spoken of the vitality of Christianity in Europe and among emigrants of European stock and Christian ancestry in the Americas and Australasia. The faith grew as well among almost all major non-Occidental peoples and among the majority of tribes of non-Europeans.

Among the Polynesians, on the eastern fringes of the islands of the Pacific, the Gospel won the majority and worked profound changes in their cultures. It was introduced into most of the other islands of the Pacific and in some made remarkable progress. The spread was mainly through Protestants, but Roman Catholics were also strongly represented. In the East Indies, which later we have learned to call Indonesia and over the larger part of which the Dutch extended their rule, Protestant Christianity made rapid progress, largely among animistic folk and chiefly through Dutch and German missions. By 1914 Roman Catholics were having substantial advances.

In general, it was among peoples of animistic religions and primitive cultures that Christianity registered its largest gains from non-Christian faiths. That is not surprising, for it was these cultures rather than the "higher" ones of Asia and its fringing islands which disintegrated the most rapidly under the impact of the Occident. Their peoples were, accordingly, more ready to listen to the message of the missionary than were those who proudly clung to their inherited civilizations and religions.

Thus in Madagascar, mostly of "primitive" and near-"primitive" cultures, among the leading people, the vigorous Hova, after severe persecutions the Christian communities, mainly Protestant, grew rapidly. The faith also made progress among some of the other tribes of the island.

In the century which followed 1815 Occidental peoples penetrated all of Africa south of the Sahara, the area where was the largest aggregation of "primitive" peoples, and European governments annexed all of it except little Liberia. The penetration and the annexations were mostly in the second half of the century. This meant that in 1914 the dissolution of the tribal structure and the old patterns of culture had only begun. During the most of the century, and especially in its later decades, missionaries, some Protestant and some Roman Catholic, established themselves in all the political units and in many of the tribes of the region. They won thousands of converts, notably in South Africa, where Protestants predominated, and in Uganda, in uplands under the Equator, where Protestants and Roman Catholics entered almost simultaneously in the wake of Stanley, the explorer who continued the labours of David Livingstone. They reduced scores of languages to writing, translated into them the whole or part of the Bible, began schools to prepare the Africans for the white man's world which was so rapidly being thrust upon the continent, and in the treatment of disease pioneered in substituting Western medicine and surgery for native witchcraft.

In North Africa and Asia, where the majority of the peoples were of "higher" civilizations and religions, Christianity, as we have suggested, made less rapid numerical headway. It was to them, however, that the majority of missionaries, Roman Catholic and Protestant, directed their efforts and they were not without success. In what may be called the Moslem world, which stretches from Morocco eastward into Central Asia and India, resistance was great and few converts from Islam were made. A few thousands were gathered into the Roman Catholic and Protestant folds, especially the former, from the older Christian churches which had been in that region before the advent of Islam and which through the centuries had offered a slowly losing resistance to that politically and numerically dominant religion. Yet through schools and hospitals, as we have hinted, something of the moral and spiritual influence of the Gospel leavened the lump of Islam.

Great gains were made in India by Roman Catholics and particularly by Protestants. They were in part numerical. It was sobering and significant, however, that they were mostly from the depressed classes and the hill tribes, both of them groups which were little if any removed from the state of "primitive" cultures. It was sobering, because it indicated that very few from the upper and dominant classes of India had been won. It was significant as indicative both of the message of the Gospel "to the poor," as Christ himself had stressed it, and because it might be the fashion, unplanned for by most missionaries, through which the Gospel would spread through the rest of India. For these underprivileged groups the Gospel proved a door of hope. It meant opportunity for schools, better physical conditions of living, and, above all, moral and spiritual advance. Much emphasis was placed by Protestants upon bringing the techniques of Western medicine to minister to the sick in India.

Even more energy and funds were devoted to schools. In this financial assistance was obtained from the British government of India. That aid was given, not because the schools were Christian, for religiously the British regime attempted to be neutral, but because they were schools, and the government was seeking to encourage education by any and all agencies which would meet its standards. Some converts were made through the Christian schools. Many of the Christian schools, too, served the converts and the children of converts among the outcastes and the tribes. A large proportion of the students in them, especially in the higher schools, were from the middle and upper levels of society and were non-Christians and remained so. The extent to which they were influenced by Christian ideals would be difficult to determine and must have varied greatly with the individual. That there was some leavening of Hinduism was clear, but Hinduism was quite willing to admit Christ as one of the incarnations of the divine if it could do so without conceding that he is *the* way rather than *a* way.

In these years were laid the foundations for the effects of the Gospel on Indian life and culture which were to be marked in the subsequent period. Indeed, they were already beginning to be seen, notably so in the Brahmo Samaj, a religious movement largely among intellectuals of the highest caste which, while remaining Hindu, gave honour and reverence to Christ.

Most important for the future of the Gospel in India was the growth of the existing Christian communities and the planting of new ones. The only one which had no marked increase was the oldest, the Syrian Church, which claimed to trace its origin to the Apostle Thomas, and even from it there emerged, through contact with missionaries from the Church of England, the vigorous and vital Mar Thoma Church. In India as elsewhere the decisive test of the missionary movement would be the issuance through it of churches which in word and life would be a continuing witness to the Gospel.

Lying to the south of India and separated from it only by a shallow strait, in contrast with its prevailing Hindu large neighbour, the island of Ceylon was predominantly Buddhist. Roman Catholics, present continuously since the sixteenth century, had by far the largest of the Christian communities. Protestantism, planted first by the Dutch and after 1815 chiefly by the English, attracted a much smaller minority. In 1914 Roman Catholics and Protestants together numbered about a tenth of the population. Proportionately they were growing more rapidly than any other religious group.

In Burma, directly to the east of Northern India and shut off from it by land by rugged mountains, the dominant people, the

51

Burmese, were solidly Buddhist. In contrast with Ceylon, where the large Christian communities had been gathered mainly from those of that faith, not many Burmese became Christians. However, extensive accessions were won from the most numerous of the non-Burmese peoples, the Karens. Until touched by the Gospel the Karens were prevailingly of "primitive" culture and of animistic religion. Christianity also made gains among some of the smaller non-Burmese, animistic tribes. The growth was chiefly of Protestantism rather than of Roman Catholicism and was mainly through American Baptists who had as their pioneer the intrepid Adoniram Judson.

At the dawn of the nineteenth century the Malay Peninsula was predominantly Moslem and the Malays who then constituted the large majority of the population continued to hold to Islam. True to the record of their fellow-followers of the Prophet elsewhere, almost none of them became Christians. By the end of the century thousands of immigrants were swelling the already substantial Chinese enclaves. Indians also came, mostly as labourers. In 1914 there were growing churches among the Chinese and some Christians among the Indians.

Siam, or Thailand, was even more nearly solidly Buddhist than Burma. While both Protestant and Roman Catholic missionaries were active, the latter since the sixteenth century, by 1914 neither had gathered more than a few thousand converts.

In the second half of the nineteenth century Indo-China was brought under French rule. Made up of four main political entities, its name indicates its cultural affiliations. The northeastern part, adjoining China, drew its civilization largely from that huge neighbour. The south-west was indebted chiefly to India. Roman Catholic Christianity had been present continuously since the sixteenth century and in spite of persecutions in the fore part of the nineteenth century had gained ground. After the French occupation had brought an end to the persecutions it continued to increase and by 1914 totalled nearly a million adherents. In 1914 there were almost no Protestants.

China presented the Gospel with one of its greatest challenges and in it by the middle of the twentieth century Christianity was to have marked triumphs and major reverses. Through most of the years between 1815 and 1914 its course was extremely difficult. The Chinese were and are the largest fairly homogeneous group of mankind. They had been the creators of a high and ancient culture. Surrounding peoples had paid them the tribute of imitation and had borrowed heavily from them in art, literature, religion, and institutions. At the dawn of the nineteenth century and until 1912 China was ruled through alien conquerors, the Manchus, who prided themselves on their espousal and support of Chinese culture and whose empire included not only the traditional China but also the even larger but much more sparsely settled bounding areas. Disdainfully resistant to the pressure of the Occident, China retained both her political and cultural independence until late in the nineteenth century. Then, reluctantly yielding to the force of Western arms and when she had become in effect a conquered and occupied country, she entered upon the first stages of what proved to be a more sweeping cultural revolution than that experienced in our era by any other major highly civilized people, unless it may be the Russians.

In the early and some of the later stages of that revolution Christianity had a very large part. Three times Christianity has been introduced to China—in the seventh, the thirteenth, and

53

the sixteenth century. Twice, succumbing to the resistance of Chinese culture, it died out. The third time, represented at the outset for two and a half centuries only by the Roman Catholic Church and then, beginning in 1807, also by Protestants, it persisted and eventually flourished. While, as was to be expected because of their more prolonged presence, in 1914 Roman Catholics were more numerous than Protestants, in that year the latter were represented by a somewhat larger body of missionaries, percentage-wise were growing more rapidly, and were touching the life of the country at more different angles. Baptized Christians then numbered slightly less than two million, four-fifths of them Roman Catholics. This was less than one in two hundred of the population.

As to methods, as we have suggested, Roman Catholics focussed their energies upon making converts and building the Church. Protestants, on the other hand, sought to approach China through many channels, more so than in any other country. Like the Roman Catholics, they endeavoured to win converts and to gather them into churches. More than in any other land large numbers sought to broadcast the Gospel, to "preach the Gospel to every creature," putting secondary the nourishing of continuing churches. That was notably the policy of the China Inland Mission, which eventually had more missionaries in China than any other one society, Protestant or Roman Catholic. Convinced that China could gain from the Occident much which was helpful, before the cultural revolution began Protestant missionaries were inaugurating schools of a Western type, were introducing Western medicine and surgery, and were trying to acquaint the Chinese with Western science and history. When, late in the 1890's, the cultural revolution was under way and the Chinese were eager to learn from the Occident, Protestant schools, colleges, and universities were for several years the institutions through which the Chinese could best obtain what they wished without going abroad. Protestants also took the initiative in promoting public health and in introducing and developing improved strains of wheat, poultry, and cattle to help meet the always pressing problems of food and famine. Through Young Men's and Young Women's Christian Associations they sought to build character. Much of this was congenial to the Confucian ideal which prevailed in China, that a religion should be judged by its achievements in producing a better life here and now, mentally, physically, and morally. Numbers of the leaders of the political revolution which overthrew the Manchu regime, including its chief figure, Sun Yat-sen, were Protestant Christians, educated in Protestant schools. We are to see later some of the questions which the triumph of Communism at the middle of the twentieth century raised about the wisdom of these methods and the purpose and effectiveness of Christian missions.

Since at least the seventeenth century the Philippines had been prevailingly Roman Catholic. This was through the Spanish occupation which was begun in the second half of the sixteenth century. A large Moslem minority, the Moros, remained in the South and there were animist tribes in the hills. In the main, however, the faith of the people was that of the Spanish type of Roman Catholicism. After the transfer to the United States, in 1898, Protestantism entered through missionaries from that country. It made rapid headway, chiefly among the Roman Catholics.

In Korea continuing Christian communities arose late in the

55

eighteenth century. At the outset they were Roman Catholic, at first through contacts with missionaries of that branch of the faith in China. Until the 1880's they suffered from recurring and at times severe persecutions. The government then entered into treaty relations with Western powers and persecution by the state ceased. Both Roman Catholic and Protestant missionaries came, the latter mainly from the United States and mostly Presbyterians and Methodists. Religiously the country presented a striking opportunity. The Confucianism long endorsed by the state was weak, Buddhism, formerly prosperous, was in decay, and the faith of the majority was a near approach to animism. Embroilment with their powerful neighbours, China and Japan, which led to occupation and (1910) to annexation by Japan, added to the sense of need. The numbers of Christians rapidly mounted. That was especially true of Protestants. The Protestant increase was furthered by the emphasis, especially of the most numerous group, the Presbyterians, upon Korean initiative in evangelism and in self-support. Schools aided in the preparation of leaders.

Japan, as is well remembered, did not open her doors to the Occident until the 1850's. For the previous two and a half centuries she had been almost hermetically sealed against the outer world. That had been by the deliberate policy of her rulers and was for the purpose of conserving her independence against Western aggression. Christian missions were feared as a tool and an opening wedge of that aggression. Accordingly Christianity had been proscribed. Yet in the South Christian communities maintained a hidden existence from the days of the prosperous Roman Catholic missions of the sixteenth century. When they again came to light, numbers of their members resumed the connexion with the Roman Catholic Church. However, several thousand refused to do so and, keeping up the customs which they had developed while in isolation, maintained an existence separate from that of any Western branch of the Church.

In the latter half of the nineteenth century Roman Catholic, Protestant, and Russian Orthodox missionaries established themselves in Japan. The Roman Catholics were from Europe and most of the Protestants from the United States. Christian churches sprang up and grew. Of these the Russian Orthodox was the smallest. In spite of the accessions from the rediscovered hidden Christians, the Roman Catholic Church did not attract as many as did Protestants. The latter were predominantly urban and wcrc mainly from professional and business elements which by close contact with Western culture, partly through mission schools, had their ties with their old culture and faith weakened. The larger Japanese Protestant bodies early attained financial self-support and with it organizational independence from the missionaries. By 1914 the Christians in Japan numbered only about one out of four hundred of the population.

At first sight this spread of Christianity outside the peoples of the Occident does not seem very impressive. The most striking numerical gains were among folk of "primitive" cultures and at the expense of animism. The accessions from the civilized peoples of Asia and from the "higher" religions were numerically insignificant, apparently scarcely a dent upon the strongholds of these ancient faiths. However, when four sets of facts are taken into consideration this appraisal must be modified.

First, we need to remember that most of the missions, especially Protestant missions, were of recent origin and in 1914 had been operating for only a very short time. Most of them had been begun in the second half of the nineteenth century. Even by the middle of the twentieth century many of them were less than a century old.

In the second place, we must realize the small size of the missionary force. In 1914, when it was larger than at any previous time, the missionaries in active service outside the Occident under all branches of the Church, Russian Orthodox, Roman Catholic, and Protestant, did not total more than 150,000 and were probably much less than that. They were a thin line over a long front in scores of countries. The sums for maintaining them supplied from the churches of the Occident were not $125,000,000 a year. Compared with the size of the armed forces of the day and with the expense of maintaining them, the number of missionaries and the expenditure were pitifully small. In view of these two facts, in their magnitude and extent the results were astounding.

In the third place, the results cannot be adequately measured by statistics, although these are impressive. In addition to what could be covered by figures there were the less tangible and the quite intangible effects. One of these was the permeation with Christian principles of cultures and movements outside the membership of the churches. At some of this we have hinted— in Moslem lands through schools and hospitals, in India through the Brahmo Samaj, and in China through such men as Sun Yat-sen. Pioneering in many lands as they did in schools and medical and nursing service, missionaries brought not only Western techniques but also, and more important, the example of selfless service. Still more significant and even less subject to the crass judgement of statistics were those in whom the Gospel had wrought the beginning of the eternal life which is its distinctive fruit and who within this present flesh in varying degrees were manifesting the radiance of that life, a slight foretaste of what the Christian hope declares will continue, unclouded, throughout eternity. Moreover, although usually feeble both in numbers and in many of its aspects, the Church was coming into being in land after land and people after people where it had not previously been. More rapidly than the churches which had been the means of their founding, the churches through which the Church was finding expression were feeling their way, often in unprecedented fashion, toward a visible unity which would witness to the deeper unity of love and faith in Christ which are of the essence of the Christian faith.

In the fourth place, as we are to see in a later chapter, in almost every land and people, what was begun in this brief era gathered momentum in the one which followed, the day in which we now are.

In addition to this record outside the Occident, we need to remind ourselves again of the vitality in Europe and the vigourous growth in the new nations which arose by emigration from the traditional Christendom.

From the standpoint of what was achieved, there is every reason for calling the years spanned by 1815 and 1914 the Great Century.

59

CHAPTER III

The World of Today

WHAT of the world of today? What are its main features? What is happening in the religious life of mankind? If we are to understand what is taking place in the worldwide Church we must see it in its contemporary setting. We need scarcely say that the day is one of great complexity. Yet the chief movements which characterize it are easily recognizable and in their main outlines can be quickly summarized.

The present day can be said to have begun in the memorable summer of 1914 with the outbreak of what we have learned to call World War I. Since then it has displayed important stages and many of its features have become more marked, but that date clearly ushered mankind out of one day into that other in which we are now living. How long today is to endure no one of us is wise enough to know. Yet we are aware, often painfully so, of what distinguishes it, sometimes sharply, from its immediate predecessor.

One of the most obvious features of today and in striking contrast with the world of yesterday is the prominence of war. From the vantage of the mid-twentieth century, in its relative peace the yesterday of the nineteenth century seems a strange and exceptional interlude in the stormy life of mankind. Often we are tempted to regard its optimistic hope of enduring world peace as deceptively illusory. The day which began in that eventful summer of 1914 has seen two global wars, the second of which engrossed more of mankind than did the first. We now look back upon the interval between the two wars as an uneasy truce marked by a paradox of minor wars and the most ambitious effort, through the League of Nations, to achieve a warless world that history had thus far seen. It was a truce in which those who challenged the peace were building up their forces while others of the former belligerents were seeking to recover from the drains of the preceding war. Then came World War II, followed in turn by another effort through the United Nations at a global structure for international coöperation and world peace, by other struggles, including one in Korea which engaged the forces of much of mankind, although not in such a total way as World War II had done, and by mounting armaments with the haunting fear of a third world war. The picture was further complicated by race tensions. These were acute in several lands, including the United States, but they were particularly intense and multiform in South Africa, in Europe in the 1930's and the fore part of the 1940's they brought death to millions of Jews, and later, through the creation of the state of Israel, they pitted Jew and Arab against each other.

A second and closely related feature of today is also in contrast with the world of yesterday. Instead of its great increase in wealth and power, its growing political and economic mastery of the globe, and the vast movement of its peoples overseas to found or augment new nations, Western Europe is impoverished and its political and economic control has rapidly declined. In general, its population continues to mount, although not at the accelerated pace of the nineteenth century, but the increase adds to the distress. Caught between the two Titans of the day, Russia and the United States, since World War II it has seemed a nearly helpless pawn, desired by both, divided between them, and in danger of complete destruction.

With the decline of Western Europe has come the revolt of the peoples whom it has ruled. Instead of the building of colonial empires which characterized the nineteenth century, our day has witnessed their progressive liquidation. The first hints of the revolt had been seen in the years immediately preceding World War I. The Indian National Congress had been organized, and partly in response to its pressure the Morley-Minto reforms had begun to give Indians a larger share in the government of their country. The defeat of Russia by Japan in 1904-1905 brought hope to non-white peoples who had believed the white man to be invincible. World War I and its weakening of Western Europe was followed by added restlessness and by concessions, usually more or less grudging, by the colonial regimes. Thus India, led by the Indian Nationalist Congress and by Gandhi, that impressive and compelling combination of Hindu and Christian saintliness in which the Hindu predominated, gained more and more self-government. The Dutch made concessions in the East Indies and the French in Indo-China. China began to throw off the yoke of extraterritoriality and tariffs dictated by Western nations.

World War II was accompanied and has been followed by a farther and much more marked recession of Western European imperialism. For the brief time of her triumph in the Far East, Japan ousted European rule from Indonesia and Burma and all but supplanted it in Indo-China. While technically remaining within the Commonwealth, which now with consideration for its non-Anglo-Saxon members omits the prefix British, India and Pakistan have become independent. Ceylon is a self-governing dominion within that Commonwealth. Burma has completely withdrawn from it. Indonesia retains only a nominal political tie with the Netherlands. The French maintain a precarious foothold in Indo-China, but only by exhaustive fighting and by granting autonomy to the constituent members of that area. Egypt is expelling the British and has challenged their condominium in the Anglo-Egyptian Sudan. Iran is seizing the vast British oil properties within its borders. In much of Negro Africa restlessness is mounting, especially against the British. China is completely free from extraterritoriality, although caught in a web of a new kind of imperialism, that of Communist Russia.

With its decline and the waning of its colonial empires, Western Europe has been swept by a wave of pessimism. This is in striking contrast with the optimism which was the dominant temper of that area in the nineteenth century. Soon after World War I there came out such books as the popularly written *The Passing of the Great Race* and the erudite and voluminous *The Decline of the West*. The pessimism deepened after World War II. Physical and nervous weariness and the depletion of economic reserves combined with a feeling of helplessness as Western Europe has seemed to be caught between the upper and nether millstones of Russia and the United States have produced a mixture of irritation and conviction of fatalistic impotence. The pessimism has found echoes in the United States, for that country, we need scarcely say, has intimate ties with Western Europe. It is not as deep as it is east of the Atlantic, but in the normally confident and hopeful United States there are apprehension and uncertainty, and that in spite of the great wealth and physical power of the nation.

In contrast with the pessimism of Western Europe is the air of hopefulness in several other parts of the World. Having achieved emancipation from the British rule to which they attributed their ills, many, but by no means all, Indians are confident that they can now proceed with the industrialization that they believe will give them the comforts of life for which they have long envied the Occident. Officially Communist Russia exudes assurance and hope and in this it is imitated by the Communists who in the late 1940's obtained the mastery of China. In both countries the forcibly inarticulate masses may be far from acceding to this optimism, but the propaganda with which they are flooded bids them to be confident that the golden age is immediately at hand and, indeed, has already begun.

An obvious feature of the world of today has been and is revolutions. Old political structures have been swept away. In Europe the ruling houses of Romanov, Hapsburg, Hohenzollern, and Savoy, long familiar landmarks, have been thrown into the discard and in their place have come, not fresh ruling dynasties, but quite new governments euphemistically designated republics. Similarly in China the Manchus were forced to abdicate. There an approach to anarchy followed under the guise of a republic, succeeded eventually by Communist tyranny. In independent India many a princely family which had governed under the protection of the British has been forced either to give up its authority or to hold it under greatly altered conditions as its state has been brought into the new republic.

More important than the disappearance of monarchs have been phases of the revolution which have altered, in many places profoundly, inherited ideas and institutions. Industrialization is no longer confined to the Occident, Japan, and a few urban centres in Asia, but is mounting in land after land. With it are coming the changes in the patterns of life which before 1914 had begun to be seen in Western Europe, the United States, and some of the British dominions. In China the cultural revolution has been proceeding at an ever accelerated pace. Shortly before 1914 two of the chief bulwarks of the Confucianism which had been dominant in shaping morals and customs for two thousand years were destroyed—the old educational system culminating in the civil service examinations and the Confucian monarchy. The Communists are undertaking the complete reëducation of the entire nation and are seeking to substitute for Confucianism their interpretation of history and their moral, social, and economic patterns. Since the Chinese are the most numerous of peoples, the Chinese Communist effort is the most gigantic effort at mass transformation ever attempted. Even that in Russia begun in 1917, huge though it is, has not involved so many millions, nor probably is it quite as drastic, for Russia was already accustomed to a monolithic government and intense regulation by the state, whereas in China there had been a minimum of control from the central authority and the maximum of local autonomy consistent with imperial cohesion. In Africa south of the Sahara the inherited tribal patterns are rapidly disintegrating and millions of deracinated individuals are being cast adrift from their ancient moorings. The defeat of Japan in World War II and the American occupation furthered changes in that proud land, but in the mid-century it is too early to know how permanent the more drastic of these will be.

The revolutions have been and are accompanied by restlessness among the underprivileged masses. In land after land they

65

are suffering from poverty, landlordism, and corruption. They feel the stirrings of a great hope that their lot and that of their children need not always be one of abject submission but that they, too, as have the privileged upper strata, can win access to more of the necessities and even the comforts of life.

A movement which has capitalized on this restlessness and these aspirations is Communism. It feeds on distress, offers a specious and pseudo-scientific explanation for it, declares that it need not always be, and makes glowing promises of its elimination if the Communist way is adopted. Ardently missionary and confident, it seeks to win the world and as part of its program attacks what it calls the exploiting capitalist classes and countries and the remnants of the colonialism of the Occident and pillories and magnifies the racial discrimination in the United States and other non-Communist lands.

As in the world of yesterday, so in the world of today the movements which are effecting all this array of changes have originated in the historic Christendom, mainly in Western Europe. They continue to be felt in Christendom. There they have produced some of the more sweeping of the political revolutions, violently so in Russia, Germany, Austria, Italy, Czechoslovakia, Hungary, and Poland, and more peacefully and less spectacularly but still drastically, in Great Britain. Progressive industrialization has increased the urban population and the contrasts beween its patterns of life and those of the rural districts where the old order more nearly persists are still striking. However, some of the social and economic revolution seen in the cities has been spreading in the villages and farms, although more slowly. So, too, in the younger nations in the Americas and Australasia which have sprung from migrations from

Europe changes are in progress. Since these lands have not been wasted by war, the changes are not as spectacular. Because of the contrast it has sometimes been said that Europe is now the New World and the Americas the Old World. Yet even in the Americas, where the patterns of yesterday more nearly persist than in Europe, alterations are being wrought in the structure of society and in attitudes of mind which are probably as basic as those on the other side of the Atlantic.

The contrast between the New World of Europe and the Old World of the Americas is made vivid by the mounting tension between Russia and the United States. The Russia of our day has been harnessed to Communism, an ideology which was developed in Western Europe and was given its determinative form by Karl Marx, mainly while living in London, that chief centre of the economic world of the industrialized nineteenth century. The masters of Russia have developed and modified Communism. Through the weakening of Western Europe and the development of the enormous natural resources of Russia under the Communist machine, that huge land has achieved the prominence which long before its capture by the Bolsheviks far-seeing prophets had predicted for it. Through a new version of imperialism, rendered more potent by the skilful disguise of high-powered propaganda of unprecedented proportions which with demonic cleverness urges Communism of the Lenin-Stalin brand upon the oppressed and underprivileged peoples of mankind as their one and inevitable hope, the rulers of Russia have succeeded in making Russia the dominant centre of a fresh kind of empire which now embraces most of the heartland of Eurasia, the largest of the land masses of the globe. From that, in a manner which seems to confirm the dreams of the geopoli-

67

ticians, they seek to reach out until they have incorporated the rest of the world.

In this ambitious program the Russian rulers have as their major opponent the United States. Because of its vast territorial extent, its unity, its enormous natural resources, and the skill with which these assets have been achieved and developed, the United States is the wealthiest and from the standpoint of physical might the most powerful nation of today. It, too, is the foremost champion of an ideology. That ideology is the kind of democracy which has been created by Anglo-Saxon peoples during the last three centuries or more. It is much older than Communism and in one or another form has been more widely adopted. In contrast with Marxist-Leninist-Stalinist Communism, which, while deeply indebted to Christianity, is openly anti-Christian, this Anglo-Saxon democracy is largely the outgrowth of the extreme form of Protestant Christianity which is usually, but somewhat loosely and inaccurately, called Puritanism. While by no means fully Christian or not even ostensibly so and espoused and supported by many who would not call themselves Christians, it does not oppose Christianity and many of its leaders honestly consider it Christian and a bulwark of the Gospel. In defense of this democracy the United States has sought and is seeking to draw together the free nations. It endeavours to do this without dominating them. Through propaganda, although not on so large a scale as that of Russia, through a variety of pacts, through economic aid, and through the United Nations and the latter's agencies it strives to bring about a voluntary association of the peoples of the world that will not only resist Communism but will also, and without tyrannical control by any party, make for the welfare of mankind and fulfil the hopes which now stir the underprivileged masses.

The world of today has as one of its most striking features the conflict between these champions and their rival ideologies. Christianity is threatened by the one and clearly has its greater opportunity under the other.

The wealth of the United States and the decline of Western Europe have placed upon the churches of the former the major responsibility for the maintenance of the Christian missionary enterprise, both Roman Catholic and Protestant, but especially the latter.

Whether through Russian Communism or through the association of free nations sponsored and encouraged by the United States, in one form or another the culture which had its origin and initial and major development in the traditional Christendom, especially among the peoples of Western Europe, continues to spread. This is in spite of the revolt of the rest of mankind against political and economic control by the Occident. Peoples formerly subject or still subject to Occidentals, while rebelling against the white man's domination, are eager to adopt whatever they believe has given the West the power and the wealth which they envy. What particularly attracts them, therefore, are the machines of the Occident and the science and technology which make the machines possible. They wish to have factories, railways, automobiles, and the other material accompaniments of Occidental civilization that they may enjoy what they believe these have brought to the West. With these enter other contributions from the Occident, some of them tangible and some less tangible. Among them are the movies, the radio, the kind of education through which the science and technical skills of the Occident are transmitted, augmented nationalism, political ideals and institutions, some by way of Russia and others from the free world, and social customs.

The problem of satisfying the aspirations of the submerged masses which underlie much of the unrest and which feed the desire for the gadgets of the Occident is complicated and made more difficult by a vast increase in population. This has been in spite of the loss of life brought by the wars of our day. Indeed, in some quarters the distress attendant upon those wars seems to have stimulated it. It has obviously been furthered by improved public health and medical care. There are other causes which are more obscure and perhaps more potent. The increase is seen in most lands, including those of the Occident. It has become particularly pressing in Asia and its fringing islands, notably and even tragically in India, Java, China, and Japan. In these lands and some others it makes more remote the satisfaction of the longing for most of the necessities and comforts of life on which feeds much of the unrest and revolution of our day.

The pressure of population on subsistence is being aggravated by world-wide inflation. In almost and perhaps every land the purchasing power of money has declined since 1914, in some countries more drastically than in others, and prices have mounted. At one time or another in Germany and China the inflation was so extreme that prices became astronomical and money eventually valueless. The problem, however, is universal and is especially acute for the poor. Incidentally, it has rendered more difficult the support of the churches and their missions, for as a rule the giving to them has not increased as rapidly as costs.

The vast changes of our day cannot fail to affect religious beliefs and life. In the world of yesterday when the movements

70

originating in the Occident had only begun profoundly to move non-Occidental peoples, their impact was felt chiefly by Christianity, for it was the faith which was most widely spread in the Occident. In the Occident Christianity has continued to be affected, but in the world of our day all the faiths of mankind have shown the results of the impact. Each has suffered, but it is significant that, although its strongholds are in the region from which the revolutionary forces have issued, namely, the Occident, Christianity is displaying much more vitality than is any of the others and, as we are to see, continues the amazing geographic spread which marked the world of yesterday. All the other religions have suffered, some of them to the point of death. None has shown a vitality which approaches that exhibited by Christianity.

In the world of our day the most obvious foe of the historic religions is Communism. As is well known, it declares religion to be the opiate of the people. Usually it professes to permit freedom of religion, but it defines that freedom in its own terms, terms which are often very restrictive. At times and places it bends its energies toward the eradication of the existing religions. At other times it tolerates religion, leaving to what it believes to be the automatic course of history the demise of the surviving cults. Yet always it is antagonistic. With its philosophy of history and its interpretation of the universe it is itself a kind of religion, and it is one which brooks no rivals. In the totalitarian organization which it imposes on a country it has enormous advantages over competitors. Where it holds sway all religions lose adherents.

Another current foe of the historic faiths, often more subtle and in some ways more dangerous than Communism, is what

71

is often termed secularism. It is the attempt to live without God. It may ignore religion entirely, it may consider it an unessential but decorative aspect of life, it may, as do some nationalists, notably in India, regard it as a handicap and even an enemy, or it may value religion as a support of morals and the established order in state and society. As an attitude it is very old, but it flourished in the world of yesterday and has become widespread in the world of our day. Various factors have promoted it. One is religious agnosticism, the conviction that the questions raised by science and philosophy have cast such doubt upon inherited religious convictions that there is insufficient ground to affirm them, but that there is still enough possibility that they are solidly based not dogmatically to deny them. Another factor is so much absorption in other interests, such as making a livelihood, business, pleasure, art, or politics, that by millions religion is either ignored or is regarded with perfunctory assent, and is dismissed with occasional attendance at a religious observance and using the offices of religion in a merely conventional fashion at such events as birth, marriage, and death. Secularism is a frequent companion of nationalism. Those who give to the nation their primary allegiance seek to make religion serve its ends, even though they may not have any confidence in the validity of religious beliefs.

Because of these foes, in the world of our day the historic religions have been dealt severe blows. In China secularism, nationalism, the impact of Western learning and political institutions, and now Communism have weakened Confucianism, seemingly fatally, have hastened the decay of Buddhism and Taoism which has been under way for centuries, and have also dealt blows to the ancient polytheism and animism. We are to

72

see later how Communism has adroitly attacked Christianity in China. In Turkey a secularist regime which came into power on the eve of World War I has handicapped all religion, even the Islam of which its predecessors, the Ottoman sultans, were official guardians. In India Nehru and some of his colleagues in the Congress Party look upon the religious divisions of India as obstacles to the integrated nation-state which they are striving to create. They see a vivid confirmation to their dislike in Pakistan, distinct politically because of Islam and halting the full unification of the country. They know that religion is too strong in India to be eradicated, unless in the far distant future, but they dislike it. In several lands the historic religions have had something of a revival because of their association with nationalism, but the seeming new life comes because a particular religion is regarded as an essential element in the culture of the nation and as strengthening the latter or as to be conserved with pride because it is part of the national heritage. This is true of Islam in Egypt and of Buddhism in Ceylon. In Japan before the defeat of that country in World War II and the compulsory disestablishment imposed by the victors, State Shinto was utilized by the super-nationalists to reinforce loyalty to the state.

A third foe to the historic religions and closely related to the other two is what is sometimes called modern mass society. It is the product of the changes brought by the mechanical appliances and the industrialization of life which had their beginnings and have had their most extensive development in the Occident. It is spreading rapidly among the rest of mankind and is having a particularly spectacular increase in Russia under Communism. Modern mass society is seen in the aggregations of labour in the factories and mines, whether in Britain,

73

Germany, Russia, the United States, Japan, South Africa, or any other country where these appear. It characterizes the modern city, with its lack of sense of community and the great housing developments with their aggregations of individuals and loosely knit families with no common bond and with little or no acquaintance with one another. It is furthered by the means of rapid transportation which make it easier for individuals to become rootless and to avoid social responsibilities. It is aided by the newer means of communication, whether by the newspaper, the telephone, the movie, the radio, or television. All these are assets to propaganda and contribute to an uncritical mass mind. Modern mass society makes for the break-up of inherited social patterns and institutions, such as the family and the religious units of other days. It also leads to the atomization of society and to a specialization with resulting occupational groups which make comprehensive community difficult. Huge organizations have arisen—of business, labour, and the state—which overshadow the churches. Wherever mass society appears inherited religious beliefs and practices, whether Christian or non-Christian, are weakened and tend to die. Yet there is also a longing for unity in the midst of diversity which affords opportunity for a world-embracing philosophy or religion.

As was to be expected from the fact that Communism arose in Europe and there has its main stronghold, that secularism in its modern forms is of European origin, and that modern mass society appeared first in Western Europe and there has had its most extensive development, these three foes of religion have dealt especially severe blows to the faith of traditional Christendom. So devastating have they seemed to be that many are speaking of the de-Christianization of Europe. The facts which they adduce to the support of this thesis are sobering. In Russia and in the lands of Europe dominated by Russia and Communism the churches have dwindled in numbers and much of the rising generation has seemingly been lost to the faith of their fathers. In Western Europe, outside the "iron curtain," the inroads of secularism and modern mass society and, among minorities, of Communism have been notable. In France, where because of the revolutions of the eighteenth and nineteenth centuries large elements have long been divorced from the Church, de-Christianization has proceeded so far among the majority, especially in the industrial centres, that the country is regarded by many as predominantly pagan and an urgent mission field. In England it is said that of the potential Protestant church membership only about one in seven are communicants and that not more than one in ten of the population regularly attend church. In Sweden, where the overwhelming majority are Lutherans, members of the state church, and where religious instruction is given in the schools, it is estimated that less than a tenth are fairly faithful in coming to the services of the Church. In Germany, as in other countries in Western Europe, the Church still has a substantial part in the life of the rural villages and towns, where the older patterns of life more nearly persist, but in Berlin it is reported that even in the Western zone, where Communism is not in command, not more than 5 per cent have much active concern for the Church. The proportion of the professedly Roman Catholic population in Germany who are faithful in attending public worship is said to be considerably larger than that of the Protestants. The decline appears to have been mainly among the latter. With such conditions in the heart of the historic Christendom, long the main stronghold of

75

Christianity, the outlook for the future of the faith might well seem to be grim.

However, as in the Christendom of the nineteenth-century yesterday so in the Europe of today the picture is one of contrasts. Now as then, if only one set of facts is taken into account, Christianity appears to be dying. Death seems to be coming first in Europe, where the forces bringing about the demise had their rise and have been longest at work. Enemies of Christianity or pessimists might well say that survivals and gains in the newer nations of European stock and outside the Occident are due to momentum from earlier, more favourable days. It might be argued that there is that in the Gospel which makes for its eventual disappearance. As evidence there could be cited the fact that the foes which seem to be winning in the struggle against the faith had their birth in Christendom and owe their existence in part to direct or indirect impulses from Christianity. We may note that this last is no new experience for the faith. One striking example is Islam. Islam arose in the seventh century, in the following two hundred years overran about half of the then Christendom (although that was an area and a population considerably smaller than what today might be given that designation), and, while latterly making few gains, except in Spain, Portugal, and Sicily has retained the ground once won and continues to be the most effectively resistant to the Gospel of all the non-Christian religions. Yet it honours Jesus, although not in the way that Christians do, and arose in part from contacts of Mohammed with Christianity.

On the other hand, although the forces adverse to traditional religions originated, have had their main centres, and have attained their greatest force in Europe, long the chief citadel of

Christianity, that faith displays greater vitality than do all of the others taken together—Judaism, Islam, Hinduism, Buddhism, and Confucianism—to mention only the more prominent of them, and, as we are to see in a moment, it continues the amazing expansion which it achieved in the world of yesterday. Indeed, the three recent major foes—Communism, secularism, and modern mass society—are not so much foes as challenges. There are indications that they are provoking the Church to a deeper understanding of the Gospel and greater efforts to witness to it and to lead all men to discipleship and to obedience to the Church's Lord. In that symbolism given by Christ of the Church as an army attacking the city of evil, it may well be that these fresh devices of the ancient foe are like sorties from a beleaguered fortress whose prince knows that his doom is already sealed and that these desperate sallies are being used by the Lord of the Church to stimulate the latter to renewed effort in the long siege whose victorious outcome has already been decided. That at least appears to be the conviction of the New Testament, a conviction which we are to amplify in a later chapter.

The evidences that the abounding vitality of Christianity has been stimulated afresh by the challenges of the world of our day are many and are seen in each of the three main branches of the Church. As in the world of yesterday, they are more marked in Roman Catholicism than in Eastern Orthodoxy, and are still more striking in Protestantism.

In the family of Orthodox Churches, that of Greece has shown real vigour. To be sure, along with the Greek people, it has suffered from the wars of the period, first from the deportation from Turkey of the Greek population after the close of

World War I and then from the enemy occupation during World War II. Yet between the two wars a movement called *Zoe* flourished, by its very name indicative of a new burst of life. Even though it has affected directly only a minority of the laity and clergy, it has persisted and has revived since liberation. Among the laity there is decided interest in the Christian understanding of history. Moreover, in the United States the Greek Orthodox Church has had and is having a striking growth. As is to be expected, its strength is among the Greeks in that country. The severe blows dealt by the Communists to the largest of the Orthodox Churches, that of Russia, have cost the latter many adherents and the majority of its clergy. However, even in Russia that church persists. For a variety of reasons, beginning in the 1940's the Communist-controlled state has lightened its adverse pressure. The surviving church buildings are reported to be thronged with worshippers. Now and again there is a convert from the de-Christianized masses. Moreover, in some places outside Russia and the iron curtain the Russian Orthodox Church is thriving. For instance, in Paris there is a centre from which has issued creative theological thought whose influence has been felt far beyond the boundaries of that communion, notably through the writings of Berdyaev, and in the United States the church has grown.

The Roman Catholic Church has had and has no easy time in the world of today. In Europe it could not and cannot help but feel the blows of the two world wars which have centred in that continent, of the totalitarian regimes in Germany and Italy which followed the first of those wars and whose anti-Christian convictions were but thinly veiled, of Communism, of secularism, and of modern mass society. We have noted that France, from which more Roman Catholic missionaries had gone in the nineteenth century than from any other one country, has become so largely de-Christianized that it is regarded as a mission field. The Roman Catholic Church has set itself firmly against Communism and the Communists have responded by regarding that church as a major enemy. In Hungary, Jugoslavia, Czechoslovakia, and Poland, all countries where Roman Catholics are either in the majority or constitute a large element in the population, the triumph of Communism has brought embarrassment and some persecution. Thousands of Uniates, those of the Orthodox Church who generations ago through political pressure were brought within the Roman Catholic fold, have returned to the Russian Orthodox Church, presumably largely under Communist constraint.

Yet the Roman Catholic Church continues to display great vigour and much fresh life in Europe, its historic citadel. In this world of today, the world since 1914, it has developed the Liturgical Movement, an effort to bring the entire congregation into conscious and intelligent participation in the worship of the mass. It has produced outstanding thinkers, such as Maritain, who command the respect of the intellectual world and who are interpreters of Christian theology to the men of the age. It has stood against the Nazis and the Fascists and continues potent in both Germany and Italy, in the latter country with a revival in its intellectual life. In France there are sacrificial and novel efforts by priests to reach and win the de-Christianized labouring classes and there are also some of the ablest Roman Catholic intellectuals. Great Eucharistic congresses, some of them in Europe, some elsewhere, have quickened the devotion of clergy and laity to Christ through the central rite of the

Church. Roman Catholic missionaries continue to go out to the ends of the earth. Even more than in the yesterday of the nineteenth century Roman Catholics tend to be a minority set in a hostile world, but it is a minority under leaders who have no thought of final defeat or of any other outcome of the struggle but eventual victory.

It may well be that the waning of Western Europe, which is presumably to continue, will disappoint this confidence, for there has been and still is the main centre of the Roman Catholic Church. After all, it is the *Roman* Catholic Church. It finds its unity through and in the Church of Rome. It is in reality the church of Latin Europe, a continuation in a religious form of the Roman Empire, and it has had and continues to have its main strength in South-western Europe, the portion of the world that was most permeated by the culture and speech of Rome. That part of the earth is clearly declining from the prominence which since the fifteenth century it has held in the life of mankind. As that decline becomes ever more marked, in spite of its world-wide spread, the Roman Catholic Church, wounded at its heart, may also dwindle. However, it still has enormous vitality in Europe and is, in the main, gaining in numbers on its geographic periphery.

It is Protestantism which, even in that ravaged Europe much of which is apostate, has shown more vigour than any other branch of the Church. It has lost in numbers, but in other ways it has gained. It has persisted behind the iron curtain. In Russia itself, almost under the shadow of the Kremlin, Protestants called Baptists and Evangelicals worship in crowded congregations. In East Germany and Hungary Christians bear their witness, consciously under the Cross. Here and there are centres of fresh devotion and vision, as yet only of minorities. In Switzerland and Sweden, countries which through their neutrality kept out of active participation in the two world wars but in which sensitive souls could not but be stirred to the depths by the agony on their borders, there have been fresh statements of the eternal Gospel. Some, seeing the impotence of man to achieve the order of which the nineteenth century optimists had dreamed, far from despairing, have stressed the initiative of God in making Himself known through His Word, the incarnate Christ, and in His act for man's redemption. Others, while not yielding a whit on the Divine initiative and the Incarnation, emphasize the self-giving love of God in the Incarnation, the Cross, and man's salvation.

In some ways still more striking has been the continued and rapid growth of the new approaches to Christian unity which were begun in the yesterday of the nineteenth century. Denominated the Ecumenical Movement, true to its name, as we are to see a little later, it is world-wide in its outreach and has taken a variety of forms. However, it has its main headquarters in Europe and has many Europeans among its leaders, in Europe it has brought into its fold a larger proportion of the Protestants than on any other of the continents, and in one way or another it has drawn into fellowship more non-Protestant Christians than in any other area of the globe. In Europe the Ecumenical Movement has led to some actual unions of churches. These have been mostly in Great Britain and bodies within the same denominational family, notably the bringing together in 1929 of the Church of Scotland and the United Free Church of Scotland and in 1932 of the largest groups of English Methodism. But on the Continent there has also been the fusion of the two wings of the Reformed Church in France. In Germany since World War II most of the Protestant churches have been drawn into a kind of federation in what is known as the Evangelical Church in Germany. In the British Isles there is a Council of Churches which embraces the Church of England, the Church of Scotland, and several of the nonconformist or free churches.

Several of the bodies which have brought together not churches but individuals from two or more churches have grown in this post-1914 age. Prominent among them have been the Young Men's Christian Associations. Although Protestant in origin and predominantly Protestant in leadership and membership, in some countries, especially after World War I, it has been prevailingly non-Protestant. Thus in Greece it is mainly Greek Orthodox and in Poland, so long as the Communists permitted it to live, its membership was chiefly Roman Catholic. Yet all these national units are kept in fellowship through a World's Committee and a World Alliance. So, too, the World's Student Christian Federation has others than Protestants in some of its units.

The year 1921 saw the organization of the International Missionary Council which had been envisioned at the World Missionary Conference at Edinburgh in 1910 but which had been delayed because of World War I. It furthers consultation and joint action by the larger part of the Protestant missionary enterprise. Also in the 1920's came the first meeting of the World Conference on Faith and Order and the Universal Christian Council for Life and Work. In the next decade these two drew together to bring into being the World Council of Churches. The constitution for the World Council of Churches was drafted in 1938, at Utrecht, the inauguration and first assembly were at Amsterdam in 1948, and the headquarters are in Geneva. Declared by its constitution to be "a fellowship of those churches which accept our Lord Jesus Christ as God and Saviour," is has as members not only the churches which include all but a small minority of the Protestants of Europe and the churches which embrace the majority of the Protestants in other parts of the world, but also several of the Eastern Churches and of the Old Catholic Churches. It and the International Missionary Council are officially in "association with" each other and work through a joint committee and it welcomes a tie with "other ecumenical bodies" such as the World Council of Christian Education and the world organizations of the Young Men's and Young Women's Christian Associations. The World Council of Churches thus becomes the affiliating centre of most of the bodies of Protestant origin which are endeavouring to knit together in fellowship all those who bear the Christian name. That fellowship is by no means complete. The Roman Catholic Church, several of the Orthodox Churches including the largest of them, that of Russia, and numbers of Protestant bodies, among them some of the largest in the United States, have not been willing to join. Indeed, a few have taken a distinctly adverse stand. Yet here, rapidly growing, is a movement, largely novel, toward unity among Christians. It has as its primary objective, not defense against the hostile forces of the world of our day, but carrying the Gospel to all men and bringing the Gospel to bear upon the life of mankind.

The Protestant movement toward Christian unity is even more marked in land after land outside of Europe. Thus in the United States there are hundreds of city and state councils of churches, most of them formed since 1914, and the National

Council of the Churches of Christ in the United States of America, constituted in 1950 of several existing national bodies for coöperation for specific purposes. In its membership are not only churches embracing the majority of the Protestants of the country, but also the Polish National Catholic Church of America and some of the American units of the Eastern Churches. In the United States, moreover, there have been several unions of churches, although entirely of those of the same denominational family, such as the United Lutheran Church of America in 1917 and 1918, the Norwegian Lutheran Church of America in 1917, the Methodist Church (1939) which fused the Methodist Episcopal Church, the Methodist Episcopal Church, South, and the Methodist Protestant Church, and the Evangelical and Reformed Church, made up of the Evangelical Synod and the Reformed Church in the United States. In Canada a more comprehensive union was achieved in 1925 in the United Church of Canada by the Methodists, the Congregationalists, and a majority of the Presbyterians. In many countries there are national bodies sometimes, as in Canada, called a council of churches and in others a national Christian council. The actual union of churches has gone further in younger countries, as the United States and Canada, or among churches more recently founded and in lands outside the Occident. Thus the Church of Christ in Japan, constituted in 1941, brings together denominations as different as Baptists, Methodists, Presbyterians, and Congregationalists. The Church of Christ in China, formed in 1927, with a strong Presbyterian nucleus, drew in some Congregationalists, some Baptists, some former Methodists, and the United Brethren. The Church of South India, consummated in

1947 and with about a million members, embraces Anglicans, Methodists, Congregationalists, and Presbyterians.

Here is a movement toward Christian unity centring in and radiating from the most divided wing of Christianity, Protestantism. Begun in the relatively peaceful yesterday of the nineteenth century, it continues to gain momentum in the stormy world of today.

In the world of today, then, Christianity, although challenged by many foes which have arisen from within its traditional stronghold, Europe, and which are spreading throughout the world, is showing amazing vitality. While in some lands it seems to be on the defensive, in most lands it is reaching out, registering fresh gains in numbers and putting its impress on the collective life. This last becomes especially apparent as we move outside of Europe and survey the rest of the globe.

CHAPTER IV

The Spread of the Gospel in the World of Our Day

ONE of the astounding and most significant facts of the world of our day is the continued spread of the Gospel, the growth of the churches which are its creation and its vehicles, and the widening and deepening impress of the Gospel on mankind. As we have said in the preceding chapter, this is quite the opposite of what might have been expected. Some of the outstanding features and forces of the age are openly or subtly enemies of the faith. Arising in Europe, the heart of the historic Christendom, they have brought numerical losses to the churches there. Yet, as we have seen, the faith is demonstrating its enduring vitality in that continent. It is even more proving its power by its performance the world around.

As in the yesterday of the nineteenth century so in our day the spread is through the three main wings of Christianity— the Orthodox, the Roman Catholic, and the Protestant. The Orthodox achievements are chiefly in the United States through strengthening the hold of the Church on the immigrants who are traditionally of that faith. Almost no gains are being made among non-Christians. The Roman Catholic Church is active in almost every country and is growing in numbers in the United States and outside the Occident. Protestants are increasing rapidly in the United States, among nominally Roman

Catholic populations in Latin America and the Philippines, and among the traditionally non-Christian peoples. Missions are more and more drawing their support from the rank and file of church members, and in Britain and the Continent of Europe the missionary enterprise has been increasingly woven into the texture of the structure and life of the churches. It already had that status in the United States and Canada.

A striking feature of the world of today is the fashion in which Christianity is becoming rooted among peoples to whom the Gospel was either almost or entirely unknown at the dawn of yesterday, a century and a half ago. We have seen (Chapter II) that in that yesterday the Gospel spread in connexion with the expansion of the economic and political imperialism of Western Europe, but that very early the purpose of the missionaries, expressly so of Protestant missionaries, was to plant self-supporting, self-governing, and self-propagating churches. In the world of our day great gains have been made toward attaining that objective.

This has been from at least three causes. One is the eagerness of previously subject peoples to achieve independence of control from the Occident. Manifesting itself strikingly in the political realm, it has, quite understandably, also expressed itself in the churches, for their members wish to be free from the taunt of being agents and dupes of foreign imperialism. A second cause is the labours of missionaries, some of them in that yesterday, but even more of them in our day, who have laid the foundations of the churches, have sought to train leaders, and in other ways have endeavoured to further the vitality of the Christian bodies which they have nurtured. A third cause, and one which is of first importance, is the power of the Gospel itself.

The universality of the Gospel has been demonstrated by its ability to call forth from every nation and people communities of those who exhibit its transforming power. Even though at present the Church is not rooted in Afghanistan, Nepal, and Outer Mongolia, this is because of adverse geographical and political conditions and is not from an inherent lack of appeal.

This rootage of Christianity outside the Occident has been a deliberate policy of all three wings of the Church who have engaged in the world mission. The one large Russian Orthodox mission outside Russia and the Occident, that in Japan, early stressed indigenous leadership and under the pressure of the political situation in the 1930's all its major church offices were transferred to Japanese. Since the year 1914 the Roman Catholic Church, with the powerful encouragement of the Popes, has emphasized the recruitment and training of an indigenous clergy, and members of this clergy have been raised to the episcopate in India, Indo-China, China, Japan, Madagascar, and Africa. One Chinese has been created cardinal. Protestants have been particularly forward in transferring administration to members of what they have called the "younger churches." In such of their churches as have bishops, these posts are more and more filled by "nationals." Principals and presidents of schools and colleges, heads of hospitals, secretaries of national Christian councils, and other responsible positions have an increasing proportion of "nationals" in them. In Ecumenical bodies and gatherings, notably those of the International Missionary Council, representatives of the "younger churches" are proportionately more prominent than the relative numerical strength of the latter would warrant. In Protestant missionary circles "younger" and "older" churches have been declared to be "partners in obedience" to the Great Commission. Latterly there is uneasiness over the distinction between "younger" and "older." More and more it is felt among Protestants that it is artificial and contrary to the inclusiveness of the Gospel, through which there is neither Jew nor Gentile, Greek nor barbarian, or, to paraphrase it in the situation of our day, neither Occident or non-Occident, East or West, and that all must plan and work together without regard to what outside the Gospel are striking differences. Here, for the first time in history, are Christian fellowships which are actually world-wide and not sectional or identified with particular cultural heritages.

Not only in leadership, but also in other ways the Gospel is taking root outside the Occident. It is beginning to find expression in hymns, art, architecture, and organization which arise from particular cultural heritages. Again and again, too, especially of late years, the Gospel is showing its power, notably through Protestantism, to spread without direct aid from the churches of the Occident. We are to see more of this as we make a rapid survey of the Church in the various continents and countries of the world.

We now turn to that survey. As we do so we come first to the United States, for here, as in the nineteenth century, the Church has had its largest numerical growth and from here, as we have said, come more and more of the funds and personnel for the world mission.

We saw in an earlier chapter the phenomenal advance of Christianity in the United States in the yesterday of the nineteenth century. This, we noted, was in the progressive evangelization of a partially de-Christianized population of Christian ancestry on the westward-moving frontier, in holding to the

89

faith the flood of immigration from Europe, in making an impress on the growing cities, and in winning hundreds of thousands among the elements which were non-Christian by heredity, especially the Indians and the Negroes.

In general, numerical gains have continued among all these phases of the nation's life. In 1900 the proportion of the population having membership in some church was reported as being 36, in 1910 43, in 1930 47, in 1940 49, and in 1951 58 per cent. Here is a continuation of what may be described as a mass conversion which has been in progress since the latter part of the eighteenth century. Most of the population is of Christian ancestry but had been in part or wholly de-Christianized. A substantial minority, of whom the largest element is Negro, is of non-Christian ancestry. The movement, it must be noted, is in marked contrast with the situation in Europe, where the trend is toward the de-Christianization of a predominantly nominal Christian population.

As we have suggested, the numerical gains in the United States are in all the facets of the challenge which confronted the Church in the nineteenth century. The westward movement of population has continued. The frontier, as that term was understood in the nineteenth century, has all but disappeared and conditions in the Far West more nearly approximate those in the East than in the day when white settlement was first being effected. However, in sheer numerical magnitude, the drift of population, especially into the Pacific Coast states, has probably never been greater than in the 1940's and 1950's. The danger of de-Christianization has been and is marked, for unless there is real conviction those who had a church connexion in their former homes may not reëstablish it in their new environment.

90

Indeed, the percentage of those having church membership seems in general to become progressively less from east to west. In 1926 it was about 62 and 63 on the Atlantic seaboard, 51 and 52 in the central states, 44 in the Rocky Mountain region, and 35 on the Pacific Coast. Yet the fact that it was almost as high on the Pacific Coast in 1926 as it was in the nation as a whole a quarter of a century earlier is some indication of the progress which had been realized in that period.

With the outbreak of World War I in 1914 the stream of immigration which on the eve of that conflict had mounted to more than a million a year was suddenly reduced to a trickle. Congressional legislation prevented it from again attaining its pre-war dimensions. This fact enabled the churches partly to overtake the task which had been presented to them by what had once seemed an overwhelming flood. That was especially true of the Roman Catholic Church and the Eastern Churches, for in recent years the majority of the nominal Christians in the immigration had been from one or another of those faiths. While after 1914 its percentage increase in membership was no more than that of the Protestant churches and perhaps not quite as large, the Roman Catholic Church grew in wealth and physical equipment. Its churches, monasteries, schools, and colleges became more prominent. The Roman Catholics of the United States took a much larger part than formerly in the world-wide missions of their church, both in personnel and in money. They also contributed substantially to the financial undergirding of the central administrative structure of their church in Rome. Although a minority, being more compactly organized than Protestants they have often been able to exert more influence in local politics and in labour unions than have the latter. Many of their clergy are confident, at least outwardly, that their church will have an ever greater share in the life of the United States. Yet for them, as for Protestants, the secularistic climate of opinion is a menace. Moreover, while accurate nation-wide figures are not to be had, it seems probable that the Roman Catholic Church is losing more members to Protestantism than it is winning from that wing of the faith. The Orthodox Churches have been gaining in numbers, wealth, and clergy. This is not by conversions from other churches but by better care of their hereditary constituencies. True to their tradition, the Orthodox Churches are organized according to the national origins of their members. The Russians and the Greeks are the most numerous, with the latter leading.

At mid-century the United States has far more Jews than any other country. Indeed, it has almost as many as all the rest of the world combined. Not many of them have become Christians. The trend is away from their ancestral faith, but toward irreligion and secularism and not toward the Church.

Percentage-wise the churches count a larger proportion of the urban population among their membership than of the rural districts. They are also stronger in the villages than in the countryside. Because they have been recruited extensively from the immigration of the nineteenth century, and especially from the latter part of that century, the hearts of the cities in the Northeast tend to be prevailingly Roman Catholic. Protestants, being largely of the older stock and prosperous, are found mainly in the suburbs. With some exceptions, the rural sections tend to be Protestant. But here and there, notably in the South, Roman Catholics are seeking to win this nominally Protestant element. Although the proportion of church members is higher in the cities than in the countryside, the cities, particularly the centres of the larger ones, present the challenge of modern mass society. This is outstanding in mining and industrial communities and in the new housing developments, both of single dwellings and of great congeries of apartments. The churches are making efforts to meet the challenge. Whether they have kept pace with it would be difficult to determine, for no recent comprehensive survey has been made.

The advance of the faith among the Indians has continued. In the quarter century between 1914 and 1939 the proportion of the Indian population who were counted as Christians rose from slightly less than a half to about three-fifths and it seems to have continued to mount. About half are Protestants and half Roman Catholics. Protestants have spent more per capita on the Indians than on any other racial group in the United States.

Negroes are about thirty-five times as numerous in the United States as Indians. The percentage of Negroes who are church members has mounted and is slightly larger than that among the whites. However, the proportion of Negro men having church membership is less than that of white men. Among both Negroes and whites the women outnumber the men in the churches. The overwhelming majority of the Negro Christians are Protestants, approximately two-thirds of them Baptists and not quite one-fourth Methodists. About nine-tenths of the Negro Christians are in purely Negro churches. This is chiefly by the choice of the Negroes themselves, for traditionally their churches have been important centres of their life and quite independent of white domination. Yet white denominations continue to spend large sums on behalf of the Negroes, chiefly on schools to aid in the education of members of that race. Roman Catholics

93

are active in missions among Negroes and while they have won only a small minority, proportionately that minority is growing more rapidly than are the Protestants. The northward migration of Negroes, chiefly to the cities, has brought fresh problems, but, in general, the churches seem to be rising to them.

Vast movements of population are an important phase of the present age in the United States. They are not merely in the traditional patterns of westward migration and of exodus from the country to the city, although, as we have said, these continue. They are also in the shifts of domicile within cities and from city to city, and in the throngs of chronically migrant labourers. Millions either have no fixed abode or change their place of residence too often to put down roots and become part of a community. Church connexions, if formed at all, are usually transient and casual. Here is a problem which more and more challenges the churches.

Yet, as we have said, in spite of the congeries of problems which have confronted Christianity in the United States, the percentage of church members in the population continues the fairly steady advance which has characterized it since the nation acquired its independence. With the exception of the 1850's and the 1890's, the proportional increase in the 1940's was greater than in any other decade in a hundred years.

Whether that increase is evidence of a corresponding greater understanding and depth of commitment to the Gospel would be difficult conclusively to prove or disprove. That much of the church membership is little more than nominal is clear, but presumably, if one may trust the testimony of observers of other generations, that has always been true. Evidence might be adduced to support the contention that the increase in membership has been accompanied by growing superficiality. Yet there are facts which appear to counter it. From 1910 to 1940, the years of World War I and its aftermath, the proportion of church members in the population was almost stationary, rising only from 43 to 49 percent in the thirty years. But, as we have seen, it climbed steadily in the 1940's from 49 to 57 per cent and in the year 1950-1951 rose from 57 per cent to 58 per cent. This seems to reflect a striking resurgence of vitality.

Additional evidence appears also to support the conclusion that, at least in late years, the advance in numbers has been paralleled by an improvement in quality. By far the largest of the Protestant denominational groups is the Baptists. They are more than half the size of the Roman Catholic Church. Their major strength is in the South, where in some states both among whites and Negroes they have the majority of all the church membership. They have spread through an earnest and warm evangelism which has appealed to the rank and file, especially of those of lower incomes and modest education. Next to the Baptists, but only about two-thirds as numerous, are the Methodists, who have also multiplied through enthusiastic popular evangelism, and are drawn from a slightly higher income and educational level than the Baptists. Next in order are the Lutherans, only a little more than half the size of the Methodists. They have their strength chiefly among those of German and Scandinavian stock and are witness to success in holding the immigrants to the faith of their Old Country ancestors. The denominations which draw primarily from those of the upper income and educational strata of the population, among many of whom church membership tends to be nominal and to compete with other interests—the Congregationalists, Episcopalians, and Presbyterians—together are only slightly more numerous than the Lutherans and are less than two-thirds as numerous as the Methodists. Proportionate growth is especially rapid among some of the minority churches, most of them of American origin, which stress a warm faith with high emotional content, strict personal morals, and staunch belief in the inspiration and verbal inerrancy of the Scriptures. An increasing proportion of the Protestant missionaries to other countries are from them and from those in the larger denominational groups who maintain a similar position. After a fairly steady increase in the fore part of the century, in the 1930's the numbers in Sunday Schools became nearly stationary and in some denominations declined. By 1947, however, a decided recovery was registered. Presumably this indicates an improvement in religious instruction. In the 1940's the number of ordained ministers seems to have shown a marked increase. Certainly the enrollment in theological seminaries has mounted sharply since World War II and the quality of the students appears to have risen with the numbers. Here is clear evidence of advance in the leadership of the churches. We must also note the emergence of many small groups for the deepening of prayer, for an understanding commitment to the Gospel, and for the exploration of what is entailed in various professions and occupations by that commitment. Physical centres for "retreats" of such groups are multiplying. Summer assemblies for concentrated study and worship are also increasing. In other words, it can be argued that the mounting tide of the mass conversion of the partially de-Christianized elements and of those who are non-Christian by ancestry which is in progress is being accompanied by an improvement in the average quality of dedication to the Christian faith.

In the United States, then, the situation is in some ways in striking contrast with that in Europe. So different is it, indeed, that it is often difficult for Christians on one side of the Atlantic to understand those on the other side. In Europe, Christians, whether Orthodox, Roman Catholic, or Protestant, are tending to become minorities and Christianity to lose the place which it recently held of being the avowed faith of the community, supported by the state. In the United States, where separation of Church and state has been the principle for over a hundred years, where de-Christianization has been threatened among those of Christian ancestry, and where large elements of non-Christian heredity, especially Indians, Negroes, and Jews, are present, the mass conversion which has been in progress for at least two centuries continues, and recently has been mounting.

This difference is reflected in the support of the world-wide Christian enterprise. Increasingly the financial responsibility for its maintenance is borne by the churches of the United States. The impoverishment of Western Europe and the hard pressures under which in one way or another all the churches of the Continent and the British Isles have suffered have combined to reduce or keep stationary the incomes of missionary organizations. Much self-sacrifice goes into their support. But for it they would have declined more sharply. Yet among Roman Catholics and especially among Protestants the responsibility for giving the Gospel to mankind rests more and more upon the Christians of the United States. Aid from the churches of the United States is going not only to Asia, Africa, and Latin America but also, especially in the years immediately after World War II, to the Christians and churches of Europe. Notable are Church World Service, in which Protestants of several denominations coöperate, and the American Friends Service Committee which, although under the control of Quakers, derives much of its funds from members of other denominations.

In Canada the situation is somewhat different from that in the United States. In the United States the Roman Catholic Church, while growing in wealth, remains a minority and its gains in numbers are much less than those of Protestants. In Canada, in contrast, the Roman Catholic Church is registering a marked advance as against a more nearly stationary Protestantism. That advance is due chiefly to a difference in birth rates. In Canada the Roman Catholic Church has, as in the United States, a strong Irish contingent, but, in contrast with the United States, it is predominantly French. The French Canadians are mainly rural and have large families. In general they are loyal to their church. That is partly because it is a symbol and tie of their group consciousness and life as against the Anglo-Saxon majority. The Anglo-Saxon stock, predominantly Protestant, much of it urban, has a lower birth rate. It may well be that before the end of the present century Roman Catholics will outnumber Protestants. French Canadian Roman Catholics are taking an increasing part in the world-wide missionary enterprise of their church. But Canadian Protestants are by no means quiescent. The two largest denominations, the Church of England in Canada and the United Church of Canada, as well as the smaller ones, among whom the most numerous are the Presbyterians, the Baptists, and the Lutherans, take a prominent part in foreign missions, and a national council of churches helps to coördinate the efforts of the large majority of the Protestants of the Dominion.

The Latin American scene is complex. Here, in several of the republics, is pulsing life. That is true of Mexico, where a revolution which is in part social and in part political has been in progress intermittently for many years. It is seen preëminently in the largest of the republics, Brazil, where the fabulous natural resources of forest, field, and mine are being tapped. It is also seen in Argentina and Chile and in the exploitation of the oil reserves of Venezuela. South America has long been called the "continent of opportunity."

Religiously, however, on the one hand is the weakness of what is in theory the dominant church, that of Rome. Nominally the overwhelming majority of population have membership in it and in most of the republics it enjoys a privileged connexion with the state. Yet, as earlier, it suffers from marked weakness, from the lukewarmness and even defection of a large proportion of those who are supposed to be members, and in some lands, notably Mexico, from open opposition and from an insufficient number of clergy and the low quality of a large proportion of such priests as it possesses. Numbers of the intellectuals have little use for it and maintain at most a nominal connexion with it. Many of Roman Catholic ancestry have not been baptized, and still larger numbers have not been given such others of the sacraments as are for the laity. Little effort is put forth to share in the world-wide missions of the Roman Catholic Church or even to reach the pagan Indians who are still to be found on the fringes of civilization. Indeed, the Roman Catholic Church in Latin America is more a liability than an asset to its communion. Many of its priests are from Europe and, latterly, from the United States, and such missions to the non-Christian Indians as exist are staffed chiefly from abroad. In numbers of missionaries sent Latin America is now the major foreign field of the Roman Catholics of the United

States. Thus personnel which could otherwise be deployed among non-Christian peoples is assigned to a nominally Roman Catholic area in which lives the largest body of members of that church outside of Europe but in which the faith is singularly anemic and requires continuous transfusions from abroad.

By contrast, in Latin America Protestantism is rapidly growing in numbers and vitality. Its gains are chiefly from the nominally Roman Catholic elements of the population. While assisted by missionaries from abroad, more and more it is producing its own leadership and is spreading through its own conviction and zeal. This is seen particularly in Brazil which, significantly for the future of Protestantism in South America, is, as we have said, the largest of the republics of that continent. Protestantism continues to grow in all the Latin American lands. Again and again its increase has been and still is in the face of persecution. Lately the persecution has been especially acute in Colombia and Mexico.

In Australia and New Zealand the years since 1914 have not witnessed any revolutionary changes in their religious life. The Australian churches have become less dependent than earlier upon the British Isles for clergy. In other words, they are standing on their own feet, or, to change the metaphor, they are becoming better rooted in the soil to which they had been transplanted. In New Zealand the growth of cities has made necessary the building of many new churches. That this has been accomplished witnesses to the vigour of the faith in that Dominion. The churches of both Australia and New Zealand have assumed more and more responsibility for missions in the islands of the Pacific. In this is added evidence of their vitality. In both lands, too, the movement toward coöperation and unity among Protestants is evident.

100

In the islands to the north and west of New Zealand and Australia Christianity is still advancing. Before 1914 most of the peoples, mainly Polynesians, in the easternmost fringe were of that faith and were sending missionaries to other islands. In our day the gain is continuing in the islands farther west. This has been marked even in the largest, New Guinea. The power of the Gospel was vividly displayed during World War II when troops from the United States were often astonished and rebuked by the examples of Christian living which they found in the islands on which they were stationed. In the New Hebrides, for instance, some in the American armed forces were so stirred by the radiant life of a local pastor that they were converted and after being discharged from the service more than one entered the Christian ministry.

Indonesia is the scene of a growth in the churches which was not halted even by the hardships of the Japanese occupation during World War II or by the fighting which accompanied the setting up of an independent republic after the expulsion of the invader and in the attempt to restore Dutch rule. The growth has been by both Protestants and Roman Catholics. Is has been especially marked among the Bataks, that vigorous Sumatran people of animistic culture who are now spreading to other parts of the archipelago. Even during the vicissitudes of World War II when they were deprived of missionaries from Europe and in the disturbances which followed that conflict, the Batak Christians increased by several scores of thousands. The Batak Christians were long entirely Protestant, but since World War II Roman Catholic missionaries have entered and have made considerable headway. The East Indian Church, a Protestant body having its origin in the early days of Dutch rule and long supported by the state, was separated from the latter in 1935

101

and was given its autonomy, but so long as Dutch rule lasted it continued to receive some financial assistance from the government. Even that has now ceased. Yet the East Indian Church has survived the loss of its privileged status and is quite obviously vital. The Japanese occupation brought the internment or death of Dutch missionaries and the nationalism and the struggle for independence which followed the end of Japanese rule has made difficult or impossible the restoration and reinforcement of the Dutch missionary body in some parts of the islands. However, among the Protestants Indonesian leaders are moving into the gap and are beginning to effect a federation of their churches.

Madagascar is an island where, as we have seen earlier, in the nineteenth century the Christian communities had grown rapidly. They have continued to grow. At present those who bear the Christian name number slightly more than a fourth of the population. Somewhat more than half are Roman Catholics. The large majority of the Protestants coöperate under the name "The United Protestant Church of Madagascar."

Africa south of the Sahara is the scene of as revolutionary movements as are to be found anywhere on the globe. The economic and social conditions under which its people live are changing so rapidly that what is written now may be outdated before it can be printed. The impact of European culture has been mounting at an accelerated pace. Africans fighting in Europe and Asia during one or the other of the two world wars brought back impressions of the white man's world, not all of them complimentary to the European. Europeans and Americans are rapidly developing the natural resources, drawing from them raw materials. From Africa, for example, comes four-fifths of the world's cobalt, nearly three-quarters of its palm oil, more than half its gold and cacao, and two-thirds or more of its uranium. In Africa are mined almost all the world's diamonds. Transportation and communication within the vast interior are being extended by auto and airplane. Great hydro-electric installations are beginning to utilize the water-power of the Congo. In places, notably in South Africa, the Africans are flocking as labourers to the cities. The old tribal patterns of life are disintegrating. The Union of South Africa is seething with interracial friction. In some other sections, particularly in the British possessions where some education has been given in home rule after European models, restlessness against the white man's domination is mounting.

Parallel with these changes Christianity is rapidly spreading. This is both by the Roman Catholic and Protestant wings of the faith, but, numerically, especially by the former. The growth of Roman Catholicism is outstanding in equatorial Africa, in the Belgian and Portuguese territories, governed as they are by Roman Catholic states, and in Uganda, a British protectorate. Roman Catholics constitute a fourth of the population of the Belgian Congo and of the adjacent Ruanda-Urundi, administered by Belgium under trusteeship to the United Nations, nearly a fifth of the population of Angola, and a little over a fifth of that of Uganda.

Protestants constitute fully a fourth of the African population of the Union of South Africa. Approximately a quarter of these Protestants are in proliferating indigenous sects. In addition, most of the white population of South Africa is affiliated with one or another of the Protestant denominations. Although only about a third as numerous as Roman Catholics, Protestants are also multiplying in the Belgian Congo. In Uganda they are about half as numerous as the latter. This means that in both the Belgian Congo and Uganda about one out of three of the population profess and call themselves Christians. In the Gold Coast, that British region where self-government has been granted, Christians, Roman Catholic and Protestant, are only about one in seven, with Protestants in the majority; the number has more than doubled in the past twenty-five years. The totals of Christians are greater in the near-by and much larger Nigeria. There Protestants are more numerous than Roman Catholics and have multiplied almost fourfold in the past quarter of a century, but the proportion of Christians is less than in the Gold Coast, presumably because of the strength of Islam in the northern portions of the country.

Even this brief survey of the numerical advance of Christianity in Africa south of the Sahara since 1914 discloses the fact that in our day a mass conversion is in progress. If it continues at its present rate, before the end of the century, in the previously animistic sections where Islam has not preëmpted the field—and these embrace most of the area and population—the majority, in some places the overwhelming majority, will bear the Christian name.

What will be the quality of this African Christianity? Will it be superficial, working very few changes in those who have a connexion with the Church? Or will there be growing nuclei of able, well-trained, devoted, and intelligently Christian leaders through whom will radiate a transforming faith which will steadily raise the level of the entire Christian community?

Some facts are sobering and seem to imply negative answers. The multiplication of Bantu Protestant sects in South Africa, now with a total of more than a million members, may be ominous. Springing from the soil, they can be interpreted as a foretaste of what an "indigenous" African Christianity will be, divorced from the steadying influence of missionaries from the "older" churches. They are a mixture of paganism and Christianity and morally and intellectually their leadership and membership leave much to be desired. Similarly several of the movements in other parts of Africa led by "prophets" in whom a tincture of Christianity is almost overwhelmed by other, non-Christian factors, including animism and rebellion against white supremacy, seem to bode ill for the future. The popularity in some sections of the Watch Tower movement, stemming from the American Jehovah's Witnesses and with prevailingly African leadership, may presage a perverted Christianity. Roman Catholic missionaries declare that when Protestants, true to the genius of their wing of the faith, put the Bible in the hands of Africans and encourage them to use their own judgement in interpreting it, such movements inevitably arise. Moreover, as education passes more and more into the hands of the government, one means of training leaders for the churches will be reduced. As we have seen, missionaries have been chiefly responsible for introducing the schools in which Africans can obtain the European learning which they must have in this new day. Most of such schools are still conducted by missions, many of them with government subsidies. However, governments are making schools one of their functions. It can be only a question of time until, with far larger financial resources than the missions, they will be maintaining and controlling the large majority of the schools. The trend of these schools will be toward secularism. The combination of teacher and pastor, which is

105

very common where schools are an aspect of the Christian mission, will disappear. Indeed, it is already beginning to do so. When the two offices are separated, that of pastor, more poorly paid than that of teacher, will tend to be filled by men of less training than the latter.

On the other hand are facts which make the picture of African Christianity more hopeful. Although they are still a small minority, very able and well trained African Christians are emerging. Some of them are Roman Catholic clergy, for their church is placing great stress upon developing an African priesthood, is giving an extended training to the candidates, and has raised at least two to the episcopate. Roman Catholics are devoting energy to elementary schools for the laity, but thus far are reserving secondary and higher education mainly to those preparing for the priesthood. Most of the Protestant schools are of elementary grade, but in the secondary and higher schools maintained by that branch of the faith laity as well as prospective clergy are enrolled. They are beginning to bear significant fruit. For instance, at the conference on Africa held under Protestant auspices in Springfield, Ohio, in the early summer of 1952, the representatives from the United States were profoundly impressed with the high calibre of the Africans. Yet the problem of training leadership, both lay and clerical, remains. It is encouraging and significant that the International Missionary Council is giving much attention to carrying through a survey of theological education in Africa which it is hoped will issue not only in concrete suggestions but also in measures to make them effective.

It is heartening to note, moreover, that in the tragic and complex conflicts between races in South Africa in which Communists, as in so many other places, are attempting to fish in the troubled waters, Christians of several races and churches are labouring to resolve the tensions. Although they have by no means removed them, again and again they have eased them. It is important, too, that in several of the political units in Africa south of the Sahara coöperation among Protestants has been achieved. For instance, in the Belgian Congo, where several Protestant bodies are represented, the majority have drawn together in the Protestant Council of the Congo and have adopted a common name, the Church of Christ in the Congo.

What we have customarily known as the Moslem world—a fairly solid block which embraces the northern shores of Africa, including Egypt, Western Asia from Turkey through Iran and Arabia, Central Asia, and Pakistan—continues to be seemingly almost unbroken by the impact of Christian missions. Indeed, in portions of it the churches have lost ground since 1914. During and soon after World War I the remnants of the Nestorian Church (also known as the Church of the East) which were found in Iran and Iraq were badly reduced by massacres by their hereditary enemies, the Kurds and Turks, deportations and massacres eliminated the majority of the Armenians in Turkey, and what was euphemistically disguised as an exchange of population all but erased the communities of Greek Christians along the shores of Asia Minor which had had a continuous existence since the time of the apostles. In Egypt the leakage persists from the Coptic Church to Islam which has been in progress since the Arab conquest over twelve centuries ago. The founding of Israel was accompanied by the displacement, often with intense suffering, of thousands of Arab Christians. Yet all the ancient churches survive, even though with sadly diminished numbers. Moreover, because of its birth rate, in spite of defections to the Moslems, the Coptic Church is holding its own numerically. Both Roman Catholic and Protestant missions are maintained. In spite of the legal restrictions which make all but impossible the winning of converts, they have persisted even in Turkey. Protestants have expanded their efforts in Arabia and have met less opposition than formerly. While still very small minorities, the Protestant communities in Iran have grown. Numbers of the Protestant bodies coöperate through the Near East Christian Council which, in turn, is a member of the International Missionary Council. The permeation of much of the Moslem world by Christian ideas goes on.

In our day India is experiencing striking changes. A participant, not entirely willingly, in two world wars, she has been the scene of intense nationalist movements which have brought about the independence of the country (1947) under two governments, the Union of India and Pakistan. Both remain within the Commonwealth which has Great Britain as its nucleus, but that is by their own free choice. Independence has not solved the basic problems of either country. Population continues to mount, especially in the Union of India, and with it famine conditions are chronic for large elements, particularly in recent years because of adverse weather. Feeding as usual on discontent, Communism has found rootage and has made striking gains in recent elections, notably in some sections in the South and in Hyderabad. Some are wondering whether it may not take over the country in the next five or six years and are seeking to prepare the churches for the conditions which such a regime would bring. The influence of Gandhi is by no means spent and there are those who are striving to carry forward his program for the betterment of the lot of the underprivileged. Fundamental alterations in the traditional society of India are in progress. Less spectacular than the political revolution, they may ultimately be even more important. For example, so far as law can do it, the disabilities of the depressed or outcaste classes have been annulled. Many years must elapse before deeply rooted practice catches up with legal enactment, but beginnings have been made. In other ways the traditional caste structure is beginning to show cracks.

In this changing India, notably in the Union of India, Christianity is displaying a striking growth and is making a mounting impact. In spite of the fact that the population of the country has increased by fully a fifth since 1914, the proportion of Christians has risen from a little more than one in a hundred in that year to more than two in a hundred. Both in total numbers and proportionately Protestants have multiplied more rapidly than Roman Catholics and each of these wings of the faith has shown a much greater growth than has the ancient and almost static Syrian Church. Yet under Protestant stimulus, as we have noted, in the nineteenth century a section of that church broke away, becoming the Mar Thoma Church: and the Mar Thoma Church is showing marked initiative.

Progress in developing Indian leadership has been registered by both Roman Catholics and Protestants. As in many other lands, the former make much of recruiting and training an indigenous priesthood, of raising up sisterhoods from Indian girls and women, and of appointing Indians to the episcopate. The large majority of the Protestants have come from the depressed classes and the animistic hill tribes. With their generation-long tradition of subservience, the depressed classes might

109

seem to provide peculiarly unpromising material, and competent leadership might be expected to be slow to emerge. Yet Protestant leadership is coming. Some of it is from the middle and upper castes, classes which have traditionally controlled society, but more and more with each decade some is from the underprivileged.

Indeed, one of the major contributions of the Gospel to India is the door of hope which it has revealed to these hitherto despised and poverty-stricken millions. Christian schools have taught thousands of them to read and so have placed in their hands the key to the gate which opens into a wider range of knowledge and economic and social self-help. In spite of the fact that so many of the Protestants are from the hereditarily underprivileged, their death rate is lower and their percentage of literacy is higher than the average for India as a whole.

The Gospel, too, continues to make for the improvement of the status of women. Through two medical schools, especially one at Vellore, it is contributing to the preparation of women physicians and surgeons. It has also stimulated the formation of rural coöperatives to improve the economic status of the very poor among the farmers.

One of the most striking and pervasive effects of the Gospel in India in our day has been through Gandhi. Gandhi came to prominence in India during World War I and, as all the world knows, was the outstanding leader in the movement which issued in independence, employed the way of non-violence, and stood staunchly for the removal of the barriers which had condemned the outcastes to hereditary poverty and obloquy. Gandhi did not call himself a Christian. He was a Hindu. Yet he was profoundly influenced by Christ. Some of his ideals

110

came from the Sermon on the Mount and among his favourite hymns were those which were frankly Christian. When an assassin brought his career to an end, a general comment among Hindus was that he had died a Christ-like death. Thus Hindus were making Christ the standard and were measuring their national hero by him. This is the more remarkable in light of the fact that according to the Hindu conceptions of transmigration and karma by which one's status in his present existence is determined by the balance of his behaviour, good and bad, in his previous incarnations, the crucifixion had been interpreted as indicating that Christ's karma was bad and that in his earlier incarnations he had been predominantly evil. In other words, not only were Indian convictions being modified and Christ being accepted as the highest standard of conduct, but Hindus were beginning to catch a glimpse, even though slight, of the meaning of the vicarious death of Christ. Through Gandhi Christ was making an impress on untold millions of Indians.

The multiform Protestant Christianity of India is drawing together through one or another of the means by which Protestants the world around are being the channel of new ways toward Christian unity. In 1923 the National Missionary Council became the National Christian Council of India, Burma, and Ceylon, and is now one of the strongest of the units of the International Missionary Council. As we have hinted, the formation of the Church of South India, finally accomplished in 1947, brought together about a million Christians—former Congregationalists, Presbyterians, Methodists, and Anglicans, with Anglicans in the majority—and is especially noteworthy for its full union of one of the branches of the Anglican communion with non-episcopal bodies. Indian Christians are taking an increasing part in the world-wide movement toward the unity of Christians. An Indian woman is one of the presidents of the World Council of Churches, and an Indian is the joint secretary for South and East Asia for the World Council of Churches and the International Missionary Council. In December, 1938, the International Missionary Council held the largest of its global gatherings at Tambaram, on the outskirts of Madras, and in the winter of 1952-1953 the Central Committee of the World Council of Churches, a world conference of Protestant youth, and the World's Student Christian Federation met in India.

Without sacrificing its essence, Christianity is beginning to find expression in ways which are peculiarly Indian. For example, after a manner long traditional in the land, the Gospel story is told to village audiences in lyric forms to the accompaniment of native musical instruments. Indigenous hymns and music are replacing importations from the Occident. Western hymns are being set to Indian tunes and metres and the Psalms are being put into Indian garb. Some of the Hindu devotional hymns have been adapted for use in Christian worship. Numbers of churches have been experimenting with a Christian *mela,* or festival. The *ashram,* an Indian form of group community living for meditation, worship, and sharing religious experience, is being extensively employed by Christians.

Fear has been expressed that in independent India and Pakistan, with Hindus dominant in the one and Moslems in the other, restrictions will be placed on the Christian minorities which would not have been permitted under the later stages of British rule. In a few localities something of this has been seen. On the whole, however, no serious opposition has been presented by either government. Indeed, in the great migrations which occurred at the time of independence, of Moslems from India to Pakistan and of Hindus from Pakistan to India, accompanied by tragic suffering, Christians won the approval of many in both the dominant religions by their unselfish ministry to the refugees. The rising threat of Communism makes many Christians apprehensive, both among the missionaries and the more alert and thoughtful Indians. Were Communism to obtain control of the country the presumption is that the Church would be treated much as it has been in other lands under Communist rule. Here and there preparations are being made against that eventuality.

Ceylon has been relatively undisturbed by the two world wars of our day. Granted dominion status after World War II, it remains within the Commonwealth to which the designation British is often prefixed. A surge of nationalism has stimulated a revival in Buddhism, for that faith is dominant in the island and by many patriots is closely associated with the prestige of their country. The population of the country has mounted rapidly and proportionately the increase in the numbers of Christians has not quite kept pace with it. Yet Christians are still about 9 per cent of the total, with Roman Catholics more than ten times as numerous as Protestants. Proportionately, however, the latter have multiplied more rapidly than the former, and even more so than the population of the island as a whole. Here, too, the movement toward Christian unity is felt and the three largest Protestant denominations, Anglican, Methodist, and Baptist, are in process of coming together in one church.

For Burma our day has been one of sudden storm but of a

113

surprising growth of the Christian communities. Until 1942 for about a generation Burma had been comparatively peaceful and prosperous. The British conquest had been completed in the 1880's. The *pax Britannica* had brought prosperity or at least comfort to many, had improved transportation, and had made for a growth in exports. Nationalistic agitation was rising and the British rulers had granted increasing self-government. Then, suddenly, in 1942 came the Japanese invasion and conquest. It was accompanied and followed by fighting. To internal resistance there was added the campaign of the United Nations to expel the Japanese. The Japanese collapse brought more disorder. Even though it was with the promise of dominion status, the British attempt to reëstablish their rule met resistance, and in January, 1948, a treaty between Burma and the United Kingdom went into effect by which the former became completely independent and did not remain within the Commonwealth. Internal disorder and civil strife followed the end of the Japanese occupation and the severing of the British tie. Fighting became especially acute between the dominant majority, the Burmese, and the largest of the minorities, the Karens. Friction between them had long been chronic and was heightened in the situation after the war.

Under these circumstances it might have been expected that the Christian communities would decline in numbers and morale, or at least remain stationary. This was the more likely since the churches were particularly strong among the Karens. Moreover, even before the Japanese invasion financial stringency in the United States, the source of the majority of the Protestant missionaries, had led to drastic reductions in the foreign staffs. However, between 1914 and 1942 the numbers of Christians, including that of the largest of the denominations, the Baptists, multiplied several fold. During the war between the Karens and the Burmese the numbers of Christians among the former increased by several thousand. Moreover, with the reduction of the missionary staff on the eve of World War II, the withdrawal of that staff during the war, and the failure after the war to restore the staff to its former strength, the churches became more and more self-reliant and moved toward carrying on without assistance from abroad.

British Malaya and Singapore fell to the Japanese in 1942, but were liberated in 1945. There, as we have seen, the strength of Christianity had not been among the Malays, who were almost solidly Moslem, but among the Indians and especially the rapidly growing Chinese population. This has continued to be true. On the whole, Christians have increased in numbers, mainly among the Chinese.

Thailand was also drawn into the maelstrom of World War II with embarrassing consequences for the Christian communities. In that almost solidly Buddhist country Christians had never been very numerous. Yet they increased somewhat.

Indo-China is the scene of a protracted and bitter struggle which is compounded of nationalism, French imperialism, the aftermath of Japanese imperialism, and the advance of Communism. Until World War II and the German occupation of France, followed as they were by the progressive Japanese control of Indo-China, the post-1914 scene had been fairly peaceful. There had been unrest as an accompaniment and sequel to World War I, and France had made some slight concessions to the rising tide of nationalism, but it was World War II which opened Pandora's box. Until then the Christian community was growing rapidly. It was overwhelmingly Roman Catholic, for Protestantism, a recent arrival, was represented by only three groups and had less than 10,000 adherents. Roman Catholics, who numbered about 1,000,000 in 1914, had increased to about 1,800,000 by 1939. The Roman Catholic Church was becoming rooted in the soil, with four times as many Indo-Chinese as foreign priests and fourteen times as many native as foreign sisters. Beginnings had been made of raising Indo-Chinese to the episcopate. World War II and its aftermath have worked very great hardship on the Roman Catholic Church as upon much of the other phases of the life of the area. That church has declined in membership by several thousand. Many Roman Catholics have perished, both of the laity and the clergy. At least one Indo-Chinese bishop has sought to gather his flock together in self-defense. The outlook continues to be grim.

The Philippines suffered severely from the Japanese invasion and occupation between 1941 and 1945. Before then marked advance had been made by Roman Catholics in putting their church under the direction of Filipinos and Protestantism had grown. After the defeat of the Japanese recovery in the churches has been rapid and Protestants have mounted in numbers.

In our day China, as we have noted, is the scene of a cultural and political revolution which the numbers of people involved, the varieties of forces at work, the complications of civil war and foreign invasion, and sweeping changes in basic ideals and institutions combine to make of greater magnitude than any that mankind has ever known. The revolution had begun before 1914 but after that year it swelled to ever larger proportions. The disappearance of the age-long Confucian monarchy early in 1912 plunged the country, unprepared, into an experiment with democratic, republican institutions which was early made difficult by debilitating wars between rival war-lords. When, in the 1920's, a degree of unity was being achieved by the Kuomintang under the leadership of Chiang Kai-shek, the interjection of Communism through Russian influence and partly under Russian direction and, in the 1930's, Japanese encroachments which issued (1937) in full-cale invasion and the occupation of much of the country in the 1940's nullified the gains. In 1945, partly through the help of the United States, the Japanese were expelled. However, the Nationalist Government of Chiang Kai-shek was so badly exhausted by the prolonged struggle that it was unable to assert itself effectively over the entire country, to check the extreme inflation, or to rehabilitate the nation's transportation system. In the meantime other features of China's inherited culture were disintegrating. The old educational system based upon the Confucian classics went and was replaced by schools whose curriculums were largely patterned on those of the Occident. Confucianism itself was passing, and China was thus losing the ethical and philosophical foundations upon which her culture had been based. The family system which was closely associated with Confucianism and which was a major stabilizing factor was being weakened. Buddhism and Taoism, long declining, were being discarded. Here was a great people, the largest fairly homogeneous group of mankind, with a culture which was one of the major achievements of the human race, cast adrift from its ancient moorings. Thus far the ideals and institutions of the Western democracies had failed to give the Chinese as a whole a sense of direction or an effective cohesion. The Chinese are a proud people. They

117

were humiliated and angered by their inability to annul foreign encroachments on their political and economic independence.

To change the metaphor, here was a cultural and spiritual vacuum. The liberal democratic ideals of the West were unable quickly to fill it. They might have done so in time had China's neighbours not sought to dominate her. Nationalism was intense among the intelligentsia but it lacked an adequate ideological basis. The intelligentsia largely faced westward and among them were tens of thousands who had studied in the United States and thousands who had been students in Great Britain and Western Europe. Christianity was spreading, as we are to see in a moment, but, while it had an influence much greater than the numbers of its adherents would have led one to expect, it was still the faith of only a small minority.

Communism has moved into this vacuum and its adherents are confident that it can fill it. By 1949 the regime of the Kuomintang and Chiang Kai-shek had completely lost the confidence of the country. To use an ancient Chinese expression, in the judgement of the majority it had forfeited the mandate of Heaven. The only viable alternative was the Communist Party. All the other parties were too small and weak to administer the nation. The Communists were supported by a well-disciplined army which had been indoctrinated with their principles. The Communist Party itself was closely integrated, had been tempered by the fires of adversity, and yet had not been weakened as had the Nationalist regime by having borne the main brunt of the Japanese invasion. Moreover, its leaders were profoundly convinced that Communism has the correct understanding of man and of history, that it must triumph, and that through it mankind will eventually arrive at the stage of a classless society in which each will contribute according to his ability and to each will be given according to his needs. By the middle of 1950 the Communists had obtained control of all the mainland of China and were prevented from taking Formosa, the last stronghold of the Nationalist regime, only by the intervention of the United States. October 1, 1949, they set up what they called "the People's Republic of China." They work in close coöperation with Russia and are intensely and volubly condemnatory of the United States.

The Communists have set about the complete reëducation and reorientation of the people of China. Here is the most gigantic attempt in history at the complete reshaping of the mind of an entire nation. The "brain-washing" of those of doubtful loyalty is ruthlessly carried through. The attempt is made to eliminate, as part of Western and especially American "imperialism," all leaning toward the democracy of the West and of attitudes which are associated with it. To replace it the Communist ideology is inculcated by the application of the methods of modern psychology and by drastic techniques of education and propaganda. Dissidents are ruthlessly liquidated. Some estimates place the numbers of executions and suicides at five million. Some would put them even higher.

Until the Communists took over the country Christianity continued to grow in the number of its adherents and in its influence in the nation. This is the more remarkable in view of the obstacles presented by the extensive civil strife, an active anti-Christian movement in the 1920's, and the Japanese occupation of a large part of the country, an invasion which began in 1931 in Manchuria and which, when it was forcibly ended in 1945, had brought practically all the seacoast and much of

119

the adjacent interior under its control. Yet Roman Catholics increased in number from about 1,500,000 in 1914 to about 2,375,000 in 1927 and to about 3,175,000 in 1939. Even in the ensuing decade, in spite of the Japanese invasion, they grew by about 75,000. Protestant communicants rose from a reported 257,431 in 1914 to 402,539 in 1924 and to 567,390 in 1936. In 1946 the total was said to have been 623,506, or an increase of about 10 per cent during the years of the Japanese occupation. In 1948 the total was given as 750,000. Both Roman Catholics and Protestants made rapid strides in the development of Chinese leadership. The former recruited many priests and nuns from among the Chinese and raised a number of priests to the episcopate. Protestants put Chinese in places of leadership in their churches, schools, hospitals, and central administrative agencies. There were numbers of Christians, mostly Protestants, in prominent posts in government, business, and education. Chiang Kai-shek himself was baptized and Sun Yat-sen, whose principles were ostensibly the guide of the Kuomintang, had been a Protestant since his young manhood. Moreover, true to the general trend within Protestantism, the National Christian Council was constituted in 1922 and brought together in coöperation the majority of the Protestants of China. What was called the Church of Christ in China came into being in 1927 and drew into its fold the Presbyterians and United Brethren, many of the Congregationalists, and some Baptists and former Methodists. The Roman Catholics also formed a national organization. From within Protestantism there sprang up indigenous movements, usually conservative theologically and warmly evangelistic. Christianity was clearly taking root in China.

120

The Communists are endeavouring to bring the churches completely under their control. They profess to respect religious liberty and the restraints which they impose are declared to be solely for political purposes. However, they have sought to eliminate all foreign missionaries, for these are from that West with which Communist China and Russia have been grappling both in the "cold war" and in the "hot war" in Korea and Indo-China. Thousands were allowed to leave when they believed their continued presence to be an embarrassment to their Chinese brethren. Others were arrested, tried, and expelled. In some instances they were tortured and imprisoned, and a few died under their hardships. By the close of the year 1954 almost none remained in China. The Communists have sought to induce Roman Catholics to constitute themselves into a church which will still be ostensibly Catholic but will be independent of Rome. In this they have had only very slight success. Cleverly adapting as a slogan an often-emphasized objective of Protestant missions to bring into being churches which are self-governing, self-supporting, and self-propagating, the Communists insisted that the Protestants cease to receive any funds from outside the country and be rid of all connexions with foreigners, and especially with Americans. They demanded that the churches join in the campaign to resist America and aid (Communist North) Korea and to denounce the alleged germ warfare of the United States. Church leaders have been subjected to reëducation to ensure that all ideals and attitudes derived from contact with the West are renounced and erased. They have been encouraged to hate America.

Under these circumstances Christianity is being subjected to the most severe testing that it has known in China in more than a century. That it is suffering losses is clear. Theological education is dwindling. Schools on which the churches relied for their educated leadership, lay and clerical, have been taken over by the government and their Christian emphasis eliminated. A similar fate has overtaken Christian hospitals. Pastors work at other occupations than their profession to obtain support for themselves and their families. Some church buildings have been diverted from their original purposes to the uses of the government and the Communist Party. There is no indication of an early end either of the Communist regime or of its restrictions on the churches. There are those who believe that Christianity will disappear from China, as it has done twice before, namely, after its introduction in the seventh century and after its reintroduction in the thirteenth century.

However, the Christian cannot believe the labours of earlier years to have been in vain. Even though the Church were to die out completely, the millions who in this life have been introduced to the eternal life which is in Christ and have passed through the gate of death into his presence have more than justified all the devotion and sacrifice which have been poured into China by men and women of faith.

Nor is it by any means assured that the Church will vanish from China. Christian communities there are still numerous and vigorous. More than once in the past sixty years their demise has been prophesied and not only has the event disproved the prediction but the churches, recovering, have mounted in numbers and vitality. In spite of the severity of the testing, it may be that this will again be the outcome. In more than one place since the Communists took over the country there have been accessions to the churches.

122

Numbers of Protestant missionaries formerly in China are struggling with the question as to why Christianity has not stood up better against the Communist tide. Is it because of weaknesses and mistakes in missionary methods? Is is because Chinese Christians have not been more firmly grounded in theology and thus more prepared to give, at least to themselves, an answer to the Communist ideology? Is it because Christians, and especially Protestants, are badly divided and cannot offer a united front? Is it attributable to the lack of accommodation to Chinese religious convictions and social customs? The question is not asked in any mood of frustrated impotence, but from a desire so to learn from the experience in China that Christians, especially missionaries, in other countries menaced by Communism may so act that they will be better prepared should the same flood come upon them as has seemingly overwhelmed the Church in China.

Here is not the place to go into the issue in detail. However, a few generalizations may be ventured which may help toward an answer. There appears, in the main, to have been no major significant difference in the viability as against Chinese Communism of the strains of Christianity which have arisen from the extremely varied denominational traditions and missionary methods. At first glance it seemed that those churches of more conservative theology and those groups, like the Family of Jesus, of indigenous origin, were holding up better than those of more liberal theology or with denominational patterns imported from abroad. However, it is not clear that the facts support this conclusion. Roman Catholics, who have stressed the Church and historic dogmas and ritual, appear to be faring no better than liberal Protestant groups. Nor does there seem to be a major

123

contrast in effective resistance between Protestant liberals and Protestant conservatives. Among both there have been those who have compromised their Christian witness. It was to be expected that, when missionaries withdrew or were expelled, those churches and movements which were least dependent on foreign funds and personnel would have a better record of survival than those which had not so emphasized indigenous support and leadership. Yet here, too, the record is not unequivocal. Nor is it clear that lack of unity has been a fatal weakness. The majority of those bearing the Christian name are Roman Catholics, fairly closely integrated through a national organization as well as under direction from Rome. They seem to have suffered quite as much as have Protestants. Indeed, there are indications that the Communists are trying to unite Protestant churches in some areas, presumably with the purpose of controlling them more adequately.

Much of the answer seems to lie in the connexion of Christianity in China with the Western influences which the Communists are determined to cast out root and branch and in the nature of the Gospel itself. Inevitably the Gospel has come to China through Christians from lands in which the churches are strong. These are mostly the United States, Canada, and the countries of Western Europe. The association of Christianity in the minds of the Communists with these lands and their culture is understandable. The hostility of the Communists is the stronger because the cultures and ideals of the West which the Communists are trying to uproot and supplant with their ideology have to some degree, even though very imperfectly, been shaped by the Gospel. The vitriolic vigour of the attack which the Communists have launched against Western "imperialism," which they broadly interpret as any form of the penetration of China by Western culture and ideals, witnesses to the large degree to which the China of to-day has been shaped by the West and to the potency of the Gospel in China. The effort which the Communists have put forth to sever the churches of China from all connexion with the churches of the West and the fashion in which, while professing to respect religious freedom, they have sought adroitly to bring them into conformity with the Communist program without moving directly against them is evidence that the Communists view them as formidable, and that in spite of the fact that Christians are only about one out of a hundred of the population of the country, Communists seem to have taken Christianity more seriously than they have Buddhism, Taoism, and the indigenous polytheism and animism, even though these have a much longer history in China and might therefore be assumed to be more deeply rooted in the culture of the land. They appear to have regarded it as more alive than these faiths and even a more serious threat than the remnants of Confucian ethics. Communist hostility, therefore, is evidence not only of the Western connexions of Christianity but also of the power of the Gospel.

We need to remind ourselves, moreover, that, if it is true to the Gospel which is its centre, Christianity cannot bring to its support the weapons employed against it by the Communists. It cannot recruit and maintain an army. It cannot seize control of the state and institute drastic, forcible liquidation of its enemies and critics. It cannot have the disregard for truth seen in Communist propaganda. Nor can it engage in a campaign of hate. These are instruments and procedures without which the Communists could not have obtained control of China or continue to

125

maintain themselves there. Christianity has as its dominant command that of love and its symbol is the cross, a continuing reminder both of the love and the seeming weakness of God. More than once in its history under pressure from overwhelming force Christianity has disappeared from areas where it had been strong. Yet always it has survived in other regions and has been carried from them until, as we have said, in our day it has become more widely spread than ever before or than any other religion or ideology, not even excepting such ancient rivals as Islam, Judaism, Hinduism, and Buddhism, or its newer rival, Communism. We need not be dismayed or discouraged by the reverses which are overtaking it in China. Our missionary methods are far from perfect, but even had they been free from flaws, almost certainly they would not have prevented the losses which Communism is bringing to the faith in China.

Additional light comes from Korea on the problem of the degree to which missionary methods are responsible for the fashion in which the churches in China have reeled under the blows dealt by Communism. Christianity in Korea has had a checkered history. So far as we know, the first converts came through a Korean of aristocratic family who had been won through Christian literature and through contacts with Roman Catholic missionaries while visiting Peking. From the beginning, as we have reminded ourselves, Christianity of the Roman Catholic type spread spontaneously and with very little assistance from the outside. It gained thousands, but repeated persecutions by the state reduced its numbers and it was seemingly on the way to extinction when, in the 1880's, the government entered into treaty relations with Western powers. Missionaries, both Roman Catholic and Protestant, were then able to labour with little or no interference from the state. The Protestants, especially the denomination with the largest foreign staff, the Presbyterians, insisted that the Koreans bear the main responsibility for propagating the faith and for the financial support of their churches. The numbers of Christians, especially of Protestants, rapidly mounted. Korean Christians displayed great zeal in spreading the faith. Yet from time to time adverse political conditions checked its growth. These political handicaps came through various stages of Japanese rule. They were peculiarly severe late in the 1930's and early in the 1940's when under the stress of its efforts to conquer China and to resist the United Nations, the Japanese Government was seeking to impose state Shinto on the Koreans and to eradicate from that country all foreign and particularly American influence. Yet the churches persisted and after the expulsion of the Japanese they revived. In South Korea, under the favouring religious tolerance of the republic set up there under American and then United Nations' auspices and protection, they have flourished and have won many converts, including some among the prisoners taken in the war which broke out in the summer of 1950. Yet in North Korea, where the churches were strong, Communist rule appears either greatly to have reduced their numbers or to have stamped them out completely. In other words, in Korea, where the tradition has been one of indigenous initiative in spreading and maintaining the faith, the losses, first from a hostile Korean regime, then when Japanese rule was adverse, and now under Communism, have been very marked, fully as much so as in China.

All this does not mean that there are not lessons which the Christian missionary enterprise can learn from Communism.

There are, and to these we must recur in a later chapter.

Still another test of missionary methods has been seen in Japan and here also it has come from the government, although not in this instance from one under Communist control. In spite of striking fluctuations in the rate of growth, after the reintroduction of the faith late in the 1850's until late in the 1930's, in each decade the total Christian community in Japan had increased. The coming of the Russian Revolution in 1917 cut off all financial aid from the mother church to the Orthodox Church, and while Japanese leadership stepped forward to take the place of personnel from Russia, there seems to have been a loss in numbers. Roman Catholics increased from about 66,000 in 1912 to about 109,000 in 1936, and Protestants from about 103,000 in 1914 to about 210,000 in 1936. While Protestant growth was numerically and proportionately greater than that of the Roman Catholics, it was not as marked as that between 1900 and 1914 and, due to adverse economic conditions in the United States, from which came most of their number, the staffs of Protestant missions declined by about a third between 1900 and 1936. All the three main branches of the Church, especially the larger Protestant denominations, were making rapid strides in transferring leadership to Japanese, and the major Japanese Protestant congregations took pride in their independence not only of foreign control but also of foreign financial aid. Coöperation among Protestants was growing, a national Christian council was formed in 1923, and Japanese Christians were taking their place in the Ecumenical Movement.

Then came (1937) the full-scale Japanese invasion of China. This was viewed critically by most missionaries, especially the Protestants. Stimulated by the government, the war tensions in

Japan mounted. Many missionaries left. To forestall compulsory action by the state, Protestants hastened steps toward union which they had already begun and early in 1941 drew together in what they called the Church of Christ in Japan, often known as the Kyodan from an abbreviated form of its Japanese designation. Into it eventually were gathered, partly under government pressure, the large majority of the Protestants. The government required all to participate in the ceremonies of state Shinto. Most of the Christians complied, accepting the official interpretation that this was purely patriotic and political and not religious.

The enlargement of the war which followed Pearl Harbor brought added embarrassment to the churches. Such missionaries from lands at war with Japan as remained were interned. Pastors as well as lay folk were required to work in the industries which supported the war effort. The government sought to bring all the churches, Roman Catholic as well as Protestant, into a reorganized National Christian Council and thus control them. Some Christians were induced to go overseas to reinforce the efforts of the government to consolidate its authority in the lands which were overrun by the Japanese armies and to persuade the peoples of these countries to coöperate in building the "Greater East Asia" which was the ostensible goal of the Japanese conquests. There were those who did so out of conviction that they were working for the welfare of these peoples and thus were fulfilling their Christian mission. In the later stages of the war hundreds of churches were destroyed by the American bombings. At the close of the war Christians shared in the extreme nervous and physical exhaustion from which millions of their fellow-countrymen suffered.

129

The war weakened the churches both in numbers and morale. Had it continued they would almost certainly have been still further reduced. All, whether Orthodox, Roman Catholic, or Protestant, suffered. The extensive self-government and self-support which they had achieved did not save them, a small minority, from grave losses and serious compromises of their faith to meet the demands of an inflamed nationalism.

After the defeat of Japan help came promptly from the churches of the late enemy lands, especially the United States. It was first of all physical relief, and then assistance in rebuilding church structures and providing supplies of Bibles and other Christian literature. Missionaries thronged in, Protestants and especially Roman Catholics. As before, the Protestants were mainly from the United States. The Roman Catholics were from many countries. As a reaction against the war years, many Japanese were willing to listen to the Gospel. This was partly because of disillusionment and loss of faith in the fevered propaganda with which they had been stimulated during the war to whip up their patriotic zeal. It was partly from curiosity to discover, if possible, the secret of the success of the United States. The numbers of Christians mounted, but not as rapidly as some optimists had hoped. At the close of 1949 Protestants were said to number about 186,000, which was considerably less than before the war, and in 1952 Roman Catholics were reported to total about 172,000, which was much more than before the war and about a 30,000 gain in the preceding three years. Thus Christians were not quite one in two hundred of the population. In spite of the withdrawal of some of the denominations, notably the Anglicans and Lutherans, the Kyodan still had about two-thirds of the Protestants. Large numbers of Protestant missionaries belonged to groups which did not join in the Ecumenical Movement, but the majority of Japanese Protestants belonged to churches which coöperated in it.

As we come to the close of this rapid survey of the geographic extension of Christianity in our day we must again emphasize the generalizations with which we began this chapter. Condensed though this account has been, and perhaps because of its very brevity, certain features of the outreach of the faith must be obvious. One is that in spite of mounting obstacles and opposition, Christianity is more widely extended geographically than ever before. While in the heart of the historic Christendom, Europe, it has experienced numerical losses, in almost every other part of the world the percentage of its adherents is greater than it was when, in 1914, the present day was ushered in by the shock of World War I. In most lands outside of Europe that growth is continuing. The exceptions are some of the countries of the Near East, and, latterly, because of the Communist dominance, China and North Korea. In Japan the shocks of World War II brought a reduction in numbers, but recovery has begun and for the Roman Catholics has brought the totals above the pre-war figures. In this global growth Roman Catholics and Protestants have shared. In some regions, notably Equatorial Africa, the increase of the former has exceeded that of the latter. In others the proportionate growth of Protestantism is greater than that of Roman Catholicism. Protestants are registering gains in nominally Roman Catholic populations, strikingly so in Latin America and the Philippines.

A second feature of our day is the fact that Christianity is being more deeply rooted among more peoples than ever before. Because, if the faith were to be planted at all it could only be through missionaries from the Occident, in that great century of the expansion of Christianity which immediately preceded our day, the propagation of the Gospel might be and often was interpreted as ecclesiastical imperialism paralleling the political imperialism which characterized the age. In land after land that has been rapidly changing. The Roman Catholic Church is recruiting and training a growing body of indigenous priests, lay brothers, and nuns, and has been raising some of these priests to the episcopate. Protestants are also calling forth an indigenous leadership and this leadership is more and more assuming responsibility for the churches and the institutions, such as schools, colleges, universities, and hospitals, which have sprung from Protestant effort. Among Protestants self-government and independence of foreign funds have also made progress.

A third development of our day is that Christians are being knit into two major world-wide fellowships. The one, the Roman Catholic Church, is very old and the patterns for its fellowship have long been fixed. In our day, however, because of its geographic expansion, it is becoming more nearly global than at any earlier time. The other fellowship, that centring in Protestantism and having most of its membership among Protestants, is relatively new and its patterns are still fluid. In one way or another the majority of Protestants have been drawn into it and in some of its manifestations it has also attracted thousands of Roman Catholics and Orthodox as individuals and several of the Orthodox and Old Catholic churches. It is growing rapidly and its leaders have a sense of adventure and expectation.

A fourth development is the widening and deepening influence of Christianity upon mankind as a whole. The Gospel is by

132

no means dominant, but much more than at the dawn of our day or than in any previous age it is making itself felt around the world. This is seen in tragic distortions of the Gospel, most spectacularly so in Communism. It is evident among outstanding leaders, particularly Gandhi, who have sensed much of its genius, have sought to embody it, and in doing so have influenced millions. It has been a major inspiration in the formation of the League of Nations and the United Nations and in many undertakings, both private and by governments, for the relief of suffering and want. It is seen in self-sacrificing, loving, radiant lives in almost every tribe and nation. It is displayed in the emerging churches in lands where they have either only recently been founded or have never before been known.

As we look into the years ahead and seek to adjust our procedures to the rapidly changing scene, it is important to note that the advances achieved in our day have been largely through the methods which were devised and employed in the world of yesterday. Here and there have been modifications and innovations, but in the main the methods of the missionary enterprise of our day are a continuation of those of the nineteenth century. Among Protestants there has been the same purpose of broadcasting a knowledge of the Gospel, of bringing into being churches which will be self-supporting, self-governing, and self-propagating, and of pioneering in meeting clamant physical, intellectual, and social human needs. When one considers over how wide an area they have been applied, it is amazing that so much has been accomplished with so small a staff supported by such limited funds. The fashion in which languages have been reduced to writing, new educational systems inaugurated, modern skills in medicine, surgery, nursing, and public health introduced, improved methods of agriculture and animal husbandry applied, coöperatives organized, and centres of rural reconstruction begun, all with a mere pittance when contrasted with the ample funds possessed by governments, is one of the most thrilling stories both of yesterday and of our day. Usually, so meagre have been the finances and so few the personnel, only demonstrations could be given of what might be accomplished through larger material resources. Again and again, never more notably than by the Communists in China, even though with a denunciation of those who had devised and begun them and in a spirit far less unselfish than that shown by the missionaries, these demonstrations have so proved their worth that they have been taken over, copied, and expanded by governments.

As we move ahead in our day these procedures call for drastic reconsideration. The impoverishment of Western Europe, world-wide inflation with the corresponding rapid rise in the cost of conducting missions, and the failure of giving to missions to keep pace with that rise, even though the giving has increased in the United States, are bringing about a reduction in the staffs. With those reduced staffs we have been attempting to maintain what was begun in a period of lower costs. Fundamental thinking and action are required and changes in methods, some of them sweeping, if we are to keep pace with the demands and opportunities of our day.

The increase in costs and the decline in the staffs of missionaries of most of the major societies and denominations have made for a loss of mobility. A large proportion of Protestant missionaries are assigned to existing institutions and organizations to maintain what was begun in days when incomes of mission boards were mounting more rapidly than prices and when it was possible to venture out into new areas and to inaugurate fresh projects. For some of the older boards giving is sufficient to make possible this adventuring on new frontiers, both geographical and in methods of approach. It is also true of several relatively new societies, most of them warmly evangelistic and theologically conservative. However, the majority of the older Protestant societies, whether in Europe or in America, are having to use all but a few of their new appointees to continue what has already been begun. The reopening of Japan after World War II was followed by the return to that land of some former missionaries and by the appointment of many new ones. Yet for the most part the staffs of societies represented in Japan before the war have not been restored to the dimensions which they had late in the 1920's. Most of the increase has been by comparatively young or quite new societies which are entering Japan for the first time. The closing of China has released personnel and funds, but most of these are being reallocated to existing commitments in other lands and only a small proportion have been assigned to fresh tasks. In general there is, in other words, for the older societies a loss of mobility which issues in a failure to move into new areas where the need and opportunity are urgent.

This decline in missionary staffs and the failure of income to keep pace with rising costs in bodies through which the major part of the growth of Protestantism outside the Occident and in Latin America has been accomplished is by no means all loss. As we have seen, except where strikingly adverse political conditions have existed, as in China, Japan, and parts of the Near East, there have been marked advances both in numbers of Christians and in self-support, self-government, and indigenous leadership. As those who believe in the unceasing work of the Holy Spirit, we can be profoundly grateful that now as from the beginning of history God is using what looks like adversity to further His kingdom. Yet as we survey the trust which He has committed to us as His fellow-labourers, we must ask afresh what He would have us do under the greatly altered circumstances of our day.

CHAPTER V

The Eternal Gospel
in An Age of Storm

A S we seek to rise to our high privilege of being co-workers with God and to ask ourselves what methods we should employ in our day, we do well to seek to discern the ways in which God is working. As we do so, we must remember, as we have reminded ourselves earlier, that the prophet has told us that God's ways are not our ways nor His thoughts our thoughts, and that as the heavens are higher than the earth, so are His ways higher than our ways and His thoughts than our thoughts. We must approach our search with humility and with the full realization that unless we are born anew of the Spirit we cannot even see the kingdom of God, that is, we cannot perceive God as reigning and the fashion in which He exercises His rule. We must always remember that the word "Christianity" never occurs in the New Testament. The term there is Gospel, "Good News." We also need to recall how our Lord's message was summarized near the beginning of Mark's Gospel. It is there stated that "Jesus came . . . preaching the gospel of the kingdom of God, and saying, The time is fulfilled, and the kingdom of God is at hand: repent ye, and believe the gospel." The Greek word translated "repent" might also be translated "change your minds." A complete reorientation is necessary if we are to believe the good news that God's reign is actually here.

137

If, however, we will keep our eyes on Christ and the record of his life, teachings, death, resurrection, and ascension, and of the coming of the Holy Spirit as seen in that first generation of Christians, we may acquire a perspective which will better help us to see God at work in our day. We do well to remember that when the Word became flesh, it was in the womb of an obscure virgin of an otherwise undistinguished village, and that when the incarnate Word was born it was in a manger, unnoticed by those whom the world called great, but announced to humble shepherds, and that when the shepherds came they found "a little baby thing that made a woman cry." We need to recall that the public career of our Lord was brief, probably at most only three years, and that he took none of the measures which prudence would seem to have directed had he wished to give permanence to his work. He wrote no book. So far as his recorded sayings enable us to know his mind, he gave little thought to an enduring organization. He gathered his intimates from those whom the world deemed obscure. Moreover, he was convinced that God's way for him was one which meant not only physical suffering, but also the spiritual agony of apparent futility, frustration, and failure. It was death on a cross. To the Jews that was a stumbling block, for it seemed utter weakness, a denial of the fashion in which they were convinced that God's power would be shown. To the Greeks, with their reliance on human reason, it appeared to be irrational, stark foolishness.

Yet after he had been born anew and had been illumined by the Holy Spirt, while through the wisdom of God men through what they deemed wisdom knew not God, Paul, Jew though he was and also familiar with the Greek mind, saw that in Christ crucified were both the power of God and the wisdom of God. He perceived that the foolishness of God is wiser than men and

138

the weakness of God is stronger than men. Paul was convinced that in the seeming weakness and folly of the Cross Christ had been the victor and that in it he had triumphed over the dark forces of evil. The mighty power of God, so Paul came to believe, was seen not only in the Cross, but also in the fact that God raised Christ from the dead, thus making him the pioneer of life.

The risen Christ did not appear to Caiaphas and Pilate, but only to his disciples, including not just the eleven but also to more than five hundred who are called "brethren," fellow disciples, and then, as to one born out of due time, to Paul. Discouraged though the disciples were and completely surprised, so much so that they could scarcely believe that their Lord was alive and that they had seen him, the fact that they were disciples made it possible for them to discern the risen Christ. Thus was their Lord's promise fulfilled that the world would see him no more, but that the disciples would see him and that to all who kept his commandments and loved him he would manifest himself.

Then after forty days came his ascension with the cessation of the type of bodily appearance which had followed the resurrection, but with the assurance of continued fellowship with him. A few days later was what the Church celebrates as Pentecost, the coming of the Holy Spirit which Christ had promised. Through the centuries since that time, what Paul declared to be the fruits of the Spirit have been apparent—love, joy, peace, longsuffering, gentleness, goodness, faith, meekness, temperance. It is upon events, movements, and especially individuals and groups in which these fruits are seen that we must seek to focus our attention if we would discern God's reign.

Again and again in the New Testament we are told of judgement. At times it is described as the judgement of God, at times as the judgement of Christ, and at other times as the seemingly automatic consequences of blindness, indifference, or deliberate disobedience. One of the functions of the Spirit is described as convincing the world of sin, because of its unbelief in Christ, of righteousness, and of judgement. As we endeavour to see God's sovereignty we must expect to find evidence of His judgement.

Yet we are assured that God is love. This must mean that judgement is dictated by love. We are also emphatically told that God sent not His son into the world to condemn the world, but that the world through him might be saved. God judges that He may redeem.

If, then, we desire to respond to our high privilege of being co-workers with God, we must attempt to perceive the fashion in which God is judging men and the ways in which His salvation is operating.

We need to remind ourselves of what seem to be the reasons for God's judgement as well as what we are told are the reasons for His redemption. We remember that God created man in His own image. Since it is His purpose to have sons and not automata, He gave men the freedom to choose whether they would do His will or, rejecting it, substitute their own will. In His law, both as seen in nature and as revealed through Moses and the ancient prophets, He made clear to men what they should do if they fulfilled His purpose for them. Christ through his words and his example set forth even more clearly God's ideal for men. Those who are his disciples are to be perfect as God is perfect. Yet, rejecting God's will for them, men have violated God's law and failed to measure up to His ideal. Because of this, because of the inexorable moral structure which

God has given the universe, misery has come upon men. Here is God's judgement. Wrath has come upon men in the forms which Paul so vividly described in the first chapter of his letter to the Romans. Because of their rejection of Him and His law, they are "filled with all unrighteousness, fornication, wickedness, covetousness, maliciousness; full of envy, murder, debate, deceit, malignity; whisperers, backbiters, haters of God, despiteful, proud, boasters, inventors of evil things, disobedient to parents, without understanding, covenantbreakers, without natural affection, implacable, unmerciful." In these is seen God's judgement. As the wages of sin they culminate in death. They have their termination in destruction. Yet "God so loved the world that he gave his only begotten Son, that whosoever believeth in him should not perish, but have everlasting life." "God commendeth his love toward us, in that, while we were yet sinners, Christ died for us." He "bare our sins in his own body on the tree." "As many as received him, to them gave he power to become the sons of God." Here is God's grace, the amazing, seemingly incredible Good News.

That God's judgement is come upon men in our day must be apparent to all who are at all familiar with the world in which we live. Paul's catalogue of the fruits of man's rebellion is tragically descriptive of what we see about us. The newspapers spread it before us on every page and the radio blares it to us. Much of it, as we have seen, has come through a perversion of what God has revealed as His ideal for men and human society. Indeed, as we need again and again to remind ourselves, the ills of mankind which in our day have attained the most colossal dimensions have arisen and spread from what we have traditionally known as Christendom, the region where the Gospel has been longest continuously represented. That is seen in wars with their equipment for mass destruction. Less spectacular but probably more destructive of the highest values of human life is the kind of society which has issued from the industrial revolution and the growing mechanization of mankind. Both the wars and the machine age are the fruits of science. Presumably sprung from the conviction that the universe is orderly, dependable, and can be increasingly known and utilized by man, a conviction which seems to have come through Christianity, science can be made to serve the welfare of man. In fact it is doing so in range after range of life. Yet, when not controlled and directed by Christian faith and love, but seized upon by selfishness and reciprocal distrust it makes for tragic woe and the debasing of men below the level of the brute creation. In that woe and that debasement is seen the judgement of God. So, too, Communism is a fanatical perversion of the Christian hope. Although denying God and the possibility of eternal life for men in the fellowship and love of God, it draws from Judaism and Christianity the doctrine that the course of history inevitably culminates in a society from which exploitation of class by class, race by race, and nation by nation will disappear, and in which each will contribute to the general welfare according to his ability and to each will be given according to his need. The terrorism, the mass enslavements, and the negation of the worth of the individual which are inescapable accompaniments of Communism are the judgement of God upon this perversion of the Gospel.

Yet it may be that Communism is also a judgement of God upon the churches for failing to live out fully what is inherent in the Gospel. They have been such imperfect witnesses to the

Gospel and its full message to all aspects of human life that sincere souls, stirred by the injustices with which the churches have appeared to be allied, have denounced both the injustices and the churches. Then, stirred by the ideals which they have seen in the Gospel, they have sought other ways of realizing them, ways which are a repudiation of the Gospel. When, as Christians, we are tempted to smug self-righteousness and to regard the judgement of God as the deserved and automatic sequel of rebellion against Him of which we are guiltless, that very smugness is a judgement upon us for our share in the common guilt. As Christ again and again reminds us, self-righteousness is more to be feared than lust and theft. That is because it is a greater obstacle to the repentance without which even God cannot save us. Had all professed Christians been alert to the perils of competitive and narrowly selfish nationalism and had they laboured to counteract and if possible remove them, seeking friendly and understanding coöperation, the wars of our day would not have come. Had all those who bore the name of Christian striven to use the multiplying machines of our day to serve man's highest gain rather than seeking through them their own material profit and power and being content with the physical comfort and aesthetic satisfaction which their products brought to them, we would not have seen the deadening exploitation of masses of men which has come in the train of the industrial revolution. We do well to remember that Karl Marx did most of his writing in London. There, in the largest city of the world, its size the fruit of the industrial revolution, and in a population the large majority of whom, including especially the ruling classes, were ostensibly Christian, he seethed with helpless wrath against the injustices which he saw about him and worked out his theory of class struggle and inculcated hatred among the underprivileged for the privileged. As he saw an established church allied with privilege and noted that the non-conforming or "free" churches drew their support chiefly from the middle classes which were deriving their wealth from the misery of the poor, it is no wonder that he regarded religion, especially the Christian religion, as the opiate of the people and that he scorned the Church as either a helpless pawn or a collaborating bulwark of the exploiting classes.

Had all Christians instead of a small minority taken seriously the spiritual vacuum in China left by the disintegration of the old order, especially Confucianism and the Confucian state and educational structure, that vacuum might have been filled through the Gospel rather than left open as an invitation to Communism. Had enough Christians responded to the opportunity presented by the changing Japan in the latter half of the nineteenth century and the first years of the present century, and had they done so in humility and with regard for Japanese nationalist sensibilities, Japan might have been diverted from the mad adventure which earlier in our day brought misery upon herself and her neighbours. In her aims and methods in her imperialistic program Japan was simply a pupil, although a clumsy one, of the "Christian" West and was attempting to do what she had seen "Christian" powers apparently succeed in doing in the preceding centuries.

We must also be aware that even sensitive and alert Christians are caught in the toils of the society in which they have been reared and in the midst of which they cannot but operate. Thus, as Shaw rather cynically pointed out in *Major Barbara,* the Salvation Army, in attempting to alleviate and remedy the horrors of the London slums obtained much of the money which made their program possible from the well-to-do who had acquired their property from the direct or indirect exploitation of those whom the Army was seeking to serve. The vacuum in China was due in part to inherent weakness in the older culture, notably in Confucianism, but its immediate cause was the impact of the Occident upon that culture. That impact came as the result of the insistence of merchants from "Christian" Britain that China open its doors to their trade. The occasion of the first war by which Great Britain sought to impose her will was the effort of the Chinese Government to prevent the debauching of its subjects by opium, at that time the chief foreign import. Very few voices were raised in "Christian" Britain against this action and a distinguished American Christian, John Quincy Adams, while not defending the traffic in the drug, declared that what he deemed the main purpose of the war, the opening of China to the commerce of the world, was fully justified. It was in the wake of this and a subsequent war for the same purpose of opening China to the commerce of the outer world and under the protection of treaties obtained through these wars that Christian missionaries established themselves in China. All, even the most sensitive Christians, are under the judgement of God for seemingly inescapable associations.

Is there only judgement? Are even the most sincere Christians powerless in the face of compromising and inevitable evil in their associations? Are we caught, as were the disciples on Good Friday, where we can seemingly do nothing but stand sadly by, watching the apparent frustration of our dearest hopes, hopes which we believe are inspired by God, with nothing left to us but to bury the dead? Must we always be led into futile compromise, as was Peter when he attempted to keep within sight of his Lord, perhaps because he thus sought to remain undetected by the hostile bystanders and be at hand to help at a crucial moment, and then ended in denying him?

The record of past days and of our day gives to these sombre questions a most emphatic and triumphant No! We need to remember that had there been even ten righteous men in Sodom that city would not have been destroyed. In the years of the heartless exploitation of the Indians in the first flush of the Spanish conquests in the Americas, a courageous spirit, significantly the first Christian minister to be ordained in the New World, Las Casas, took the lead, gave heart to others, with them succeeded in having protective laws put on the statute books, and then did much to encourage their enforcement. What at the outset was a small minority, spear-headed by that earnest and radiant Evangelical, Wilberforce, brought to an end the international trade in Negro slaves and later achieved the emancipation of the slaves within the British Empire. When the vast majority of the Christians of Britain were indifferent to the challenge which their growing empire presented to them, William Carey, an obscure self-educated pastor in an inland town, had the vision, the courage, and the faith which, used by God, were a creative impulse in what eventually was one of the mightiest missionary advances in history and in India set in motion currents of life which are still mounting. When the only crack in the door which closed China to Protestant missionaries was purely commercial establishments at Canton, one man, Robert Morrison, had the divine temerity to take advantage of it. When the shipmaster from whom he obtained passage to

Canton cynically remarked, "And so, Mr. Morrison, you really expect to make an impression on the idolatry of the Chinese Empire," Morrison replied, "No, sir, I expect God will." The event proved Morrison to be right. The physically frail Hudson Taylor felt the burden laid upon him by God of China's millions who were dying without a knowledge of the Gospel. With no organization to back him, for he had severed his connexions with the inept one under which he had gone to the Far East, he prayed concretely for volunteers and funds and presented to others China's spiritual needs. As a result there came into being the China Inland Mission, which eventually was the means of sending to China more missionaries than any other one society, whether Roman Catholic or Protestant. Less than a hundred years ago, a Swiss Protestant layman, Henri Dunant, stirred by the suffering on an Italian battleground, set in motion what has become a vast international agency for the relief of distress, the Red Cross. We do well to remind ourselves what issued from the devotion of Dwight L. Moody. A country-bred lad of slight formal education, he gave himself fully to God, and there are few places on the planet which have not borne witness to the results. They include a great church and Bible school in Chicago, the Student Volunteer Movement for Foreign Missions, thriving Christian schools at Mt. Hermon and Northfield, a succession of summer conferences from which have come for two generations impulses that reach to the ends of the earth, the mission of Grenfell to the fishermen of the bleak Labrador coast, many other movements and institutions which have contributed to the present and eternal welfare of untold thousands, and millions of transformed lives.

We could lengthen this chapter indefinitely with examples of

147

men and women of our own day who, stirred by God's Spirit, venturing out in faith, have been the pioneers in movements which even now are evidence of the redeeming power of God through the Gospel. From what has come from similar lives in earlier generations, we can be confident that the fruits are only now becoming apparent and that they are to grow in whatever days may follow ours. We think of a Norwegian bishop who inspired his fellows to resist the Nazi conquerors. We recall a German nobleman and landowner who, imprisoned by the Nazis because of his loyalty to the Gospel and later imprisoned and tortured by the Russians, came through unembittered, appreciating the meaning and power of the Cross, and has been the moving spirit of vast concourses of Germans to hear the proclamation of the Gospel. We note with humble gratitude a Scot of aristocratic lineage who, impressed by the spiritual needs of his native land and especially of the partially de-Christianized masses in the great cities, has set in motion a movement which, taking as its symbol and its centre the island from which much of the evangelization of Scotland was achieved more than a thousand years ago, has planted itself in the heart of the great cities of that land, thence to seek to permeate all life with the Gospel. In Johannesburg, where the race tensions of South Africa between white and African and the physical and moral poverty of the uprooted Bantu are most acute, for nearly a generation an American missionary has been an inspirer, director, and counsellor of efforts which seek to ease the strains and to better the lives of bewildered victims of the greed of white men who have used their labour to extract the gold from the deposits of ore on which the city is built. A Japanese of gentle rearing who in his youth, as an immigrant to the United States, knew to his grief the discrimination against his people on the West Coast, and who, after becoming a distinguished educator in his native land, was forced out by the militarists because of his stand against them, returned after the defeat of Japan to head successively two universities, the oldest and the youngest, which have sought to bring the spirit of Christ into the intellectual currents of that land. These are among those who have risen to prominence. In addition there are millions who are known only to a few—and to God—who are living witnesses to the "excellency of the power of God" in "earthen vessels."

All this is what we should expect from the fashion in which the Gospel came into the world through the manger in Bethlehem and the seeming defeat of the Cross. God continues to give men a measure of free will that He may have sons and not robots. Men continue to misuse that gift, to the tragic marring of themselves and their fellows. Indeed, they pervert the very Gospel by which God seeks to save them. As, in the familiar parable of old, the husbandmen abused those whom the owner sent to collect his share of the fruit and ended by killing the master's son, so today some of the insights and the fruits of the Gospel are twisted to man's hurt and the ancient evils of mankind attain their most colossal dimensions through peoples which have been longest exposed to the Gospel. This need not surprise us. The Son of God was crucified by the official representatives of the highest religion and the best government that man had known, themselves in part the gift of God to men. The Cross was the judgement of God on man's best. God continues to judge men, as He did through the incarnation and the Cross and through the fruits of their rebellion in what Paul called "the works of the flesh," among them "uncleanness, laciviousness, . . . hatred, variance, emulations, wrath, strife, seditions, . . . envyings, murders." He judges all men, including those who bear the name of Christ. But He judges that He may save and His salvation is apparent to all who have the eyes to see. Never has it been as widespread as in our day. The eternal "Good News" was never more potent than it is now.

As those to whom is given the high privilege of being co-labourers with God, we must seek to ally ourselves with all who are the channels of His Spirit and must ask ourselves what means He would have us employ in our day to make most effective our coöperation with Him.

CHAPTER VI

As We Rise to the Challenge
of Our Day

WHAT is the call of God to us who are privileged to be His co-workers in our day? What would He have us do? What procedures of yesterday would He have us continue? What changes does He wish us to make? What innovations would He have us introduce? In one way and another each of us must wrestle with the answers to these questions. Especially must those of us who are Protestants do so. As Protestants we believe in the priesthood of all believers. We hold, with the inspired prophet, that Christ has made every Christian a priest to God, and this implies direct access to the Father. It entails responsibility as well as privilege. A priest is not only one who through divine appointment has direct access to God, but he has that access on behalf not merely of himself but for others as well. Because we are imperfect none of us can discern all of God's will in all its details. None of us should say that his answers are without error and therefore final. In giving us a measure of free will God trusts us to struggle with the problems of our day. He knows that we will differ among ourselves as to the right solutions. Yet He wishes us "to agree to differ and resolve to love." The suggestions set forth in the ensuing pages, therefore, make no claim to infallibility. If they are presented somewhat dogmatically that is because they not only represent profound conviction but also are intended to provoke thought and, it is hoped, action. They are meant to be a part of what in our day is being called an "ecumenical conversation," an exchange of thought among all members of Christ's Church that together we may discern the mind of Christ and, discerning it, may embody it in deeds.

One aspect of our day which must govern all our searching for answers is urgency. The proclamation of the Gospel has ever been urgent. The time allowed us is always brief. Each moment souls are passing out of this life without so much as having heard that there is the Gospel. The slogan coined in a high moment of yesterday, "the evangelization of the world in this generation," has enduring validity. It means that each generation of Christians has the obligation and the privilege of presenting the Gospel to each and all of their contemporaries. Impossible though that may seem of attainment, it must still be our minimum goal. But in our age Christians face an added urgency. The challenges which we outlined in an earlier chapter brook no delay. They are seen spectacularly in the advance of Communism. They are acute in the threat of a third world war. They are slightly less obvious but fully as significant and pressing in the vast ground-swell of the revolution which is moving the masses to demand more of the good things of life. In some countries, as in India, Indonesia, China, and Japan, this is made more intense by the rapidly mounting increases in populations with their highly competitive pressures on subsistence. In some, notably in Africa and in parts of the United States, the ground-swell finds expression in resentment against race discrimination and the dominance of the white man. Even more dangerous to the highest in men is the mechanization of life and the kind of mass society produced by the machine. Closely related to this last is the more subtle but still more deadening secularization which is spreading with the impact of the Occident in which it had its rise and where it has its most extended expression. Events are moving at an accelerated pace. We who are the trustees of the Gospel cannot delay if untold millions are not to be destroyed or marred. Even though we fail Him, God will not be defeated. He will always continue to call men into His service. But, so much of free will has He given to us as to all men, His purpose may be delayed if we are dilatory or faithless.

If we are adequately to meet the urgent challenges of our day we must, more than ever before, heed the summons to what has been called "mission and unity." The Church, both in its constituent congregations and as a whole, must give itself to mission. Each local church must think and act in terms of its immediate neighbourhood and of the entire world. Every Christian must be a missionary. He must realize that he has been commissioned by God to witness to the Gospel and to make it effective in one or more aspects of life. If that mission is to be performed as God meant it to be, there must be true unity among Christians. That unity is one of love. It will express itself in visible organizations, but organizations in themselves cannot achieve it. Behind the façade of what purports to be union through inclusive ecclesiastical structure there are often vast rifts caused by jealousy, self-seeking, and pride. True unity arises from humble gratitude for the love of God in Christ. It is described in the petition of Christ for those who believe on him through the word of the disciples: "That they all may be one; as thou, Father, art in me, and I in thee, that they also may be one in us: that the world may believe that thou hast sent me."

153

The purpose of that oneness is mission—that the world which crucified Christ may believe and be saved.

In spite of the amazing progress which we have noted in an earlier chapter, this oneness, this unity is far from being fully achieved. In addition to the historic rifts between Roman Catholics and Protestants and between both these and the ancient Eastern Churches, an increasing proportion of the missionaries from the "older churches" are from bodies which do not join in the many coöperative enterprises or in the Ecumenical Movement. Moreover, indigenous divisions are appearing in the lands of the "younger churches." We have still far to go before giving the united witness of faith and love.

The call to mission and unity will seem to many a futile dream. We long and pray that it will be fully met. We are challenged by the Communist parties with their driving sense of mission, their professed confidence in victory, and the ties which seem to bind them and their members together in a world-wide fellowship whose object it is to hasten and complete the revolution which Communism preaches. Yet in contrast with Communism, the churches which are the vehicles of the Gospel seem pitiably weak and hopelessly divided and the large majority of their members are apathetic. We think of congregations which we know, some of them large, well organized, and thronging the services of their churches, but with little or no awareness of needs outside their own neighbourhood and most of their members passive even in their own communities. Or we recall small churches, discouraged and on the defensive. We remember the lack of coöperation and the competition among churches even in a single community and the quarrels which rend congregations. We cynically or despairingly, even though wistfully, view the ideal of mission and unity as unattainable.

Before we allow ourselves to become discouraged by the comparison we do well to remind ourselves that behind the seeming unity of the Communist parties and the apparent submission to direction from Moscow there are many rifts, that leaders in other lands are by no means always submissive to the Kremlin, and that such unity as exists is maintained by frequent purges, some of them with attendant cruelties which Christians who are true to the Gospel could not impose on their fellows. We must also recall that a larger number of Christians are today actively committed to missions than at any earlier time in the history of the Church. For many centuries the spread of the faith was by professional missionaries. The rank and file of the laity had little interest in them or their work and gave almost nothing toward their support. Near the close of the eighteenth century, however, as we have noted, this began to change. Although they are still a minority, millions of Christians now contribute of their means and through their prayers to the world mission of the Church. That minority seems to be growing and to be larger than ever before. Some denominations officially and openly declare themselves to be missionary societies and seek to enlist all their members in intelligent participation. Moreover, as we have seen, in our day Christians are coming together to a larger degree than at any time since the first few centuries.

While all of this is true and is heartening, we of the Christian Church have much to learn from Communists. If they can be zealous and as nearly united for a cause which at best is a perversion and distortion of the Gospel and which omits and denies its very heart, how much more should Christians, entrusted as we are with the wonder and fullness of the Gospel, seek unitedly to acquaint all men with it and to embody it in individual and collective living.

We must also remind ourselves that as Communism seeks the complete transformation of society in accordance with its patterns, so we as Christians can aim at nothing less than the permeation and remaking of society in accordince with the standards given us in the Gospel. It would seem that this is implied in the declaration that "God sent not His son into the world to condemn the world, but that the world through him might be saved."

We must ever be aware that Christ pictured his Church as besieging and attacking and not on the defensive. We have better ground for confidence in the final outcome of history than do the Communists. We must not wait to act until all Christians are enlisted in the support of the missionary enterprise, for that will not be within the lifetime of any of us. We must act now and in coöperation with as many as possible.

In view of the mounting financial cost of conducting the missionary enterprise on the newer geographic frontiers and of the changes in the world situation which we have more than once summarized, we must have a thorough reëxamination of the existing methods and investment of lives and money. Thus far in our day, as we have reminded ourselves, in what we have called the "foreign field" we have been largely continuing the methods and institutions which were devised and created in that yesterday of magnificent achievement. Some of them should be carried on. But, as we have said, we do not have the staffs and the funds from what—although we have seen that that designation is something of an anachronism—we may still describe as the "older churches" to maintain them at their existing dimensions and to move out into new areas. We are in imminent danger of becoming confined to existing patterns, of losing momentum, and of approaching the condition where the "younger churches" will be self-contained minorities, not reaching out to the non-Christians about them. Of this the ancient Syrian Church in South India is a striking example. For centuries it was almost a distinct caste, neither losing to the surrounding paganism nor gaining adherents from it. Something of that danger is seen in Europe where Christianity is ceasing to be the faith professed by the majority and is becoming that of minorities who are tempted to resign themselves to that position. It is also apparent in some of the "younger churches" in Asia.

While in the lands of the "younger churches" the witness to the Gospel must more and more be by those churches, because they are often small minorities personnel must continue to come to them from the "older churches" to stimulate and reinforce them in reaching the majority about them. It is the contributions of the "older churches" which require reëxamination. They must encourage the retaining and, where needed, the regaining of mobility in fulfilling the mission of the Church to reach those who are either completely untouched or only slightly touched by the Gospel.

This reëxamination does not necessarily mean the abandonment of existing institutions and methods. It does mean, however, that they must be tested to see whether they are contributing sufficiently to the mission of the Church in our day to warrant their continuation, especially when that means that new ones cannot be undertaken or that advances into new territories, whether geographical or in areas of life, cannot be made.

Educational institutions must especially be scrutinized. In many areas the majority of the foreign personnel are absorbed by them. In the lands of the "older churches" numbers of schools and colleges founded under Christian auspices, still professing Christian allegiance and a church connexion and appealing for funds on that ground, have become so secularized as to differ little if at all from those that are frankly secular. Every school and college which wishes to retain the name "Christian" must from time to time ask afresh what being Christian means and must reëxamine its program to see whether it can honestly be given that designation. If this is necessary in lands where a large proportion of the population professes to be Christian, it is still more imperative in lands where only a small minority make any pretense of bearing that name. There schools, colleges, and universities begun under Christian auspices are in danger of becoming secularized much more rapidly and extensively than in countries which are sometimes called Christian. That is especially the case since the "younger churches" are too small to support them financially or to produce enough educators to staff them or sufficient students to fill their halls. In many of these institutions the majority of the faculty and a large majority of the student body are frankly non-Christian. Their effect on most of their students is not conversion but either the weakening of all religious faith or a shallow syncretism, an unintelligent attempt to combine the Gospel with other religions, an effort which denatures both the Gospel and its rivals. In some "Christian" schools and colleges the financial need is so great that tuition-paying student bodies are increased far beyond the proportion between teachers and students which ensures good academic work. Often the Christian institutions are academically inferior to government institutions.

The only reasons which can be put forward for continuing aid to these largely secularized but professedly Christian schools are, first, that in them some Christian influence is exerted, even though very slight, and thus preparation is made for an eventual acceptance of the Gospel, and, second, that among a people where the demand for education is great and existing facilities are quite inadequate for meeting it, funds from missionary societies make possible additional schools, even though these are little or no more distinctively Christian than are those maintained by the government or by non-Christian private agencies.

It is highly doubtful whether support for such institutions should be maintained. It is clear that they should not have first priority on the funds and personnel of missionary agencies. Either they must become much more distinctively Christian in teaching staff, student body, and program or aid to them must be shifted to agencies or areas which will yield larger returns in the spread of the faith.

It will take no small degree of courage to apply these tests. Pressure from alumni and from teaching staffs, including missionaries, to continue appropriations and to grant larger funds will be great. In many instances it will be difficult to determine whether the contribution to the Christian cause, even when not as much as desired, is sufficient to warrant further assistance. Yet we have reached the stage where courageous, decisive action is needed. Either a school or college must present evidence of being distinctly Christian or such aid in funds and personnel as is given it must be directed into other channels. We must also remember that schools which are genuinely Christian are still very much needed and can make an important, indeed an indispensable contribution to the Church and its mission. Where continued they must be in as close association as possible with the churches, drawing students from them and making it natural for graduates to return to them to share in their life.

Hospitals and medical service must also be scrutinized. If they fill an obvious void that would not be taken care of by the state if they were discontinued, they should if possible be maintained. Or, even though there are other hospitals, if those aided by the churches are vivid exemplars of Christ-like love and service they may well be supported and strengthened. Here and there, however, are probably hospitals which do not meet either test.

We must be prepared for the taking over of schools and hospitals by governments, or, at the minimum, the assumption by governments of the main burden of education and medical service. We have so long been accustomed to schools, hospitals, and dispensaries as part of the program of missions that when the state overshadows them or makes them impossible the adjustment is painful. Yet with the increase of nationalism with its resentment of foreign-controlled or even foreign-aided institutions and with the continued growth of the totalitarian state, we must be so ready for that eventuality that when it comes the churches through which the Gospel is expressed will suffer as little as possible.

Institutionalism is not confined to schools and hospitals. Churches also become institutions and we, whether of the "older" or the "younger" churches, tend to become absorbed in maintaining and operating them and to lose the sense of abandon and adventure which are of the essence of the Gospel.

Ideally Christians are a pilgrim people, strangers in this world who are seeking a city. We should be consciously living between the times—the time of the incarnation, the cross, and the resurrection, and the time of the culmination of history in the coming of Christ in glory. Even now, if we have really been born anew, we will be bearing the first fruits of the Spirit as members of God's kingdom. Yet too often the churches in which we congregate become religious clubs, largely conforming to this world and seeking to live safely and respectably in it.

Much of the missionary personnel in the lands of the "younger churches" is occupied in administration, in keeping the ecclesiastical machinery moving. As rapidly as possible these duties should be turned over to members of the "younger churches." Mission property should also be transferred to the "younger churches." Yet all of this should be done in such fashion as not to burden the leaders of the "younger churches" beyond their ability or so to engross them in maintaining the churches as institutions that they, too, lose the sense of being pilgrims and of reaching out with the Gospel to the non-Christians about them. In spite of the progress which has been seen, we have not completely solved the problem of the relations between the "older" and the "younger" churches. The two are not yet merged in one world-wide fellowship of love.

The drastic reappraisal of the use of foreign personnel and funds does not mean that all of them will be diverted from education and medical services. Schools that are truly Christian must go on. If they are to be worthy of the name they must be pioneering in new ways and must be technically not only the equal of the best of the non-Christian schools but, even more, be out in front, both in quality of instruction and in new ideas

161

and methods. They will require teachers who have the best training possible, whether they be from the "older" or the "younger" churches.

Especially do we need to stress preparation for the ministry. This does not imply that all theological education should be on the university level. Most of the ministers will have more modest academic attainments. It does mean that much more thought and resources in personnel and funds must be devoted to that branch of education than Protestants have hitherto given it in the lands of the "younger churches." This involves not reproductions of what is customary in the "older churches" but fresh experimentation in forms of the ministry adapted to particular situations and which are within the financial ability of the "younger churches" to support. It also entails new kinds of organization for the effective "cure of souls." Textbooks and other literature must be prepared, often in tongues in which no or almost no theological writing exists. Theological training in English opens a wealth of literature to students of other languages and cultures, but the ideas contained in that literature are usually expressed in terms which make no contact with the experience and thoughts of those whom the students are to serve. If they are to be communicated effectively it must be in the vernacular and in some fashion students must be helped to make that accommodation.

The personnel and funds released by the closing of institutions which are deemed not to be of sufficient aid to the Gospel to warrant their continuation and by the transfer of administration to members of the "younger churches" can be so utilized as to regain mobility. But that mobility must be through representatives not only of the "older churches" but also of the

162

"younger churches." In some areas, both geographic and of new approaches to current problems, the missionaries from the "older churches" will need to take the lead, simply because none of the "younger churches" is as yet in the area. Yet wherever possible "older" and "younger" should be joined in partnership, and in geographic areas where there are "younger churches" those sent by the "older churches" should work under their direction and in such fashion that the sense of difference between the two dies. Already in some areas "younger churches" are taking the initiative. Thus on the Gold Coast a British missionary was asked by the "young church" to become pastor of a large, well-established congregation, a post considered desirable by African ministers, that the African pastor might be released for evangelism in a hitherto untouched area.

The mobility must always have evangelism as its primary aim. The word "evangelism" needs definition. It comes, of course, from "evangel," which is derived from the Greek word of which "Gospel" or "Good News" is the English translation. It must be, therefore, at a minimum, the presentation of the "Good News," the eternal Gospel. We often limit it to preaching or we broaden it somewhat by making it mean seeking to win individuals to personal commitment to Christ. If it is to be true to the Gospel evangelism must include every means in which we can be co-workers with God in demonstrating and making effective the "Good News" of God's love in Christ. It is our high privilege to be the instruments through which the Holy Spirit touches the lives of men through the Gospel. That includes the proclamation of the Gospel by the spoken word and the printed page. It also embraces the many ways through which God's love, while respecting the free will which He has given us, seeks to permeate all the relations of men with one another. We must seek to be channels for the Gospel in every one of the multitudinous aspects of human society. This clearly includes, for instance, emphasis upon the Christian family, Christian nurture in the family, and aid in achieving a Christian family life. Again and again, as we have suggested, in many lands, both in the Occident and outside the Occident, Christians have led the way in attacking the evils which beset mankind and have pioneered in positive measures, as in education, agriculture, rural life, and public health, for improving the conditions under which men live. Measures and institutions inaugurated by Christians have been taken over by governments or by private agencies with much larger financial resources than these trail-blazers could command and in the process have been secularized. As part of their mission of evangelism Christians must continue to dare to venture out in new ways to meet human needs, even though the procedures which they devise and the organizations which they create may later be appropriated by those who do not share or share very little in the motives and the faith which have impelled and sustained them.

Herein lies a continuing necessity of winning individuals to a personal commitment to the Gospel. It is imperative not only for their own enduring welfare that individuals be introduced here and now to eternal life, but also that a constant and if possible a growing stream of those who bear the fruits of the Spirit flows into institutions and movements inaugurated by Christians to hold them to their Christian purpose. If schools, hospitals, and projects for relief and social service begun by Christians are not to lose their Christian character, they must be staffed by those in whom the Christian faith is dominant.

Closely related to the importance of what we often call personal evangelism to ensure that institutions and movements begun by earnest Christians do not cease to be expressions of the Gospel, is the challenge to make government agencies and private business enterprises which reach out beyond the borders of a particular nation channels for evangelism. This is particularly an opportunity, indeed, what should be a compelling opportunity, to the Christians of the United States. The rapid growth of the overseas activities and commitments of that nation has multiplied the number of Americans who are serving abroad. Many of these are earnest Christians. Ways must be found to relate them more actively to the world mission of the Church. They must be made familiar with what is being done by Christians in the lands to which they go. They must be encouraged to help in whatever ways are open to them. Perhaps special conferences, in the nature of information, training, and fellowship, can be arranged for them. This could be done through the boards to whom is assigned the oversight of the foreign work of the various denominations. Through such Christians the agencies of the United Nations and the various channels through which the United States Government is seeking to lift the economic level of underprivileged areas and groups in other nations can become expressions of Christian faith and service. All too often they are now staffed by personnel whose manner of living is in contradiction to the Gospel. Yet this need not be. The quality of the impact can be changed, and to the furtherance of Christian ideals.

In evangelism we must take advantage of the new means of mass communication. Not only must we make even larger use than in the past of the printed page and other visual aids, but we must increasingly bring to the service of the Gospel the radio and, eventually, television. Instances are already on record of Christian groups springing up from a hearing of the Gospel on the radio without physical contact with a missionary.

But no matter how great the use we make of these new methods of communication we must never let them be a substitute for the distribution and, where that has not been done, the translation of the Scriptures. Here must continue to be a major feature of evangelism.

If we are to rise adequately to the challenge of our day in what we may call the lands of the "younger churches" those of the "older churches" must take to heart suggestions which have been put forward again and again across the years, especially in recent decades. Efforts have been made to put them into effect, but even more than before the situation demands continued attention to them and unremitting endeavour to rise to the standards which they rightly set up.

One group of suggestions has to do with the recruiting, preparation, and attitudes of missionaries sent by the "older churches." Most of them should be so obvious that a brief enumeration is all that is necessary. Yet that is essential, since we have by no means fully attained to them.

First of all, only the choicest members of the "older churches" should be chosen. To represent the Gospel in another land and among alien peoples and cultures demands the very best in ability, devotion, and training. Those sent should be men and women of earnest Christian commitment with a personal experience of the Gospel and an eagerness to share it. They must know the Bible and be able to use it. They must be firmly grounded in an intellectual understanding of the Christian

166

faith. They must be men and women of prayer. They must have sound physiques, nervous stability, a record of financial integrity, a saving sense of humour, and proven ability to work well with others under conditions which strain tempers and physical and nervous reserves. They must be free from race prejudice and from the kind of pride in their own nation and culture which makes them disdainful of others. No technical training can be a substitute for these qualifications.

Missionaries must also have the best preparation possible in the specialty which they represent. If they are clergymen they must be familiar with the disciplines associated with that calling. If they are teachers, physicians, or nurses, they must be thoroughly equipped in their profession. More and more requests come for specialists. No short-cut or slipshod education should be tolerated. Only the best is good enough to present and apply the eternal Gospel.

Moreover, if missionaries are to communicate the Gospel adequately, they must know the language, history, religion, culture, and current problems of the people to whom they go. Here is no short-term assignment. Here is a lifetime study. Normally it should be begun before arriving in the country and it should be continued as long as residence in the land is maintained. This seems almost axiomatic, but it is not easily accomplished. The pressure of the day's tasks are such, the magnitude of what is to be done so great, and personnel are so few that all too often a missionary is so soon and so heavily loaded with burdens that he has only the sketchiest knowledge of the language and of the background and minds of those whom he has come to serve.

Then, too, closely connected with the knowledge of the coun-

167

try, its language, beliefs, and customs is the value of some familiarity with sociology and anthropology and the issues associated with contacts between cultures, especially those brought by the impact of the Occident.

The missionary has always to face the problem presented by differing standards of living. If he comes from the United States, what to him seem necessities are luxuries to most of those among whom he lives. The mechanical equipment of the home in which he was reared, with its electric lights, telephone, refrigerator, plumbing, bath and toilet facilities, and washing machine, which he has come to regard as indispensable, is beyond the reach of all but the wealthy. His salary, modest though it is by American standards, is princely compared with the income of the majority of those among whom he has come to live and of all but a very few of his colleagues of the "younger churches." It is also higher than those of his fellow-missionaries from the Continent of Europe and the British Isles. What is demanded if his witness to the Gospel is to be effective? No quick or easy answer is possible. But it should be clear that, whatever the answer, the missionary must seek to identify himself as fully as possible with the people among whom he lives.

Missionaries, especially those from the relative security of the United States, must be prepared for life in a revolutionary age, with its perils, its austerities, and its opportunities.

In our day the missionaries as well as the leaders of the "younger churches" must make themselves familiar with Communism, its beliefs, its organization, and its methods. They must be acquainted with the charges brought by Communists against Christianity and must be prepared to deal with them. They must know the main tenets of Communism and have intelligent answers to them. They must define and seek to give reality in practice to the Christian alternative to Communism. In heroism, devotion, and simplicity of living they must outdo the Communists. It was said of the early Christians that they out-thought, out-lived, and out-died their critics and adversaries. That must be true in our day of representatives of the Gospel as contrasted with the Communists.

At first sight these requirements for the preparation of missionaries seem appalling. Most of them have long been held up as the ideal. To attain them fully would consume at least half a lifetime and middle age would have been reached before they had all been met. Few have approximated to them. Yet there have been some who have met them, have done so while still young, and in doing so have proved that they are by no means impossible.

The flow of missionaries should not be one way, from the "older" to the "younger" churches. Already some from the "younger churches" have rendered outstanding service among the "older churches." A few have been pastors of local congregations. Others have specialized, some on writings which have been widely circulated among the churches of the Occident, and some as itinerant preachers and lecturers for longer or briefer periods, often in colleges, universities, and theological seminaries. Moreover, some "younger churches" are sending missionaries to lands outside the historic Christendom. Thus the Lutherans of South India are sending representatives to aid their fellow-Lutherans among the Bataks in Sumatra and Filipino Protestants are interested in Indonesia and Okinawa.

Not only must missionaries be encouraged to go from the "younger churches" to the lands of the "older churches," but the process, already begun, of the achievement by the "younger churches" of self-government, self-support, and self-propagation must continue. More and more Christianity must become rooted in every people and every land. In organization and methods it must adapt itself to each local environment and modify them as the environment changes. It must appropriate whatever of art, music, customs, and tradition can be made to communicate and symbolize the Gospel. Yet this must be done without compromising the Gospel. The Gospel must be made to penetrate all aspects of life. This can be partly through appropriate acts of worship, as when God's blessing is invoked in public ceremony on the planting of the field and thanks are given to Him for the harvest.

In this rootage missionaries from other lands can assist, but it must be achieved primarily by the indigenous churches. Once the pioneer task of planting the Church is achieved, the function of the representatives of the "older churches" is, rather, to hearten the "younger churches," to assist in training their leaders, to aid them in reaching out in evangelism, to help keep them in touch with Christians of other lands, to help knit them into the world-wide Christian fellowship, and to keep them from so conforming with their environment that they will cut themselves off from the main historic currents of Christian life in other lands and compromise the Gospel. In this manner the churches and their members in many different lands and peoples are being knit together in a world-wide fellowship in which all share actively and not passively.

Can we and will we rise to the challenge which our day presents to us as Christians? It is sobering and even staggering. We know the weaknesses of the churches of which we are mem-

170

bers. We can be reasonably sure that only a minority of those who bear the Christian name will recognize the challenge and endeavour to rise to it. Yet we can be among that minority. We must encourage minorities, both in the "older" and the "younger" churches, to gather into small groups for the study of the Bible and for prayer. We must seek to inculcate the principle of stewardship. We are aware of our own personal inadequacy. Yet we must also remember the promises and heartening assurances that are recorded in the Scriptures. "He that believeth on me, the works that I do shall he do also; and greater works than these shall he do." "If a man love me, he will keep my words: and my Father will love him, and we will come unto him, and make our abode with him." "My strength," so the Lord said to Paul, "is made perfect in weakness." Out of his experience Paul declared: "I can do all things through Christ which strengtheneth me." We must remember those of earlier days who in that faith achieved the seemingly impossible. We can also be grateful for those of our own day who, "perplexed but not in despair," are venturing forth in faith and in whom the divine promises are even now being fulfilled. We must ever rest upon the assurances given by God and upon the clarion declaration which the risen Christ gave to the disciples as he laid upon them the breath-taking command, still seemingly unattainable, "Make disciples of all nations, baptizing them . . . teaching them to observe all that I have commanded you," namely, "lo I am with you alway, even unto the end of the world." As we remember the promises we can thank God and take courage. God the Father Almighty is the maker of heaven and earth. God has not abdicated. "God is love." Trusting in His power as seen in His love, in quiet confidence in Him we can venture forth on the mission with which He has entrusted us.

171

CHAPTER VII

What Can We Expect?

WHAT can we expect as the conclusion of the story? Is the Gospel ultimately fully to triumph? If so, when and how will that triumph be? Will it come through a continuation of the historical process much as we have thus far known it? Will it be through a sudden, dramatic end of the course of history? Will it be through a combination of the two? Or will it be through steps and by means which have already been with us and which, because we do not see as God sees, we have not been clear-eyed enough to discern?

Past experience as we have briefly outlined it in the preceding chapters may throw some light on possible answers. Part of this is in the seeming paradox which we have noted as characterizing the yesterday of the nineteenth century and our own day. On the one hand is the repudiation of Christianity by much of Christendom, the strange perversion of the Gospel through movements issuing from Christendom, among them secularistic humanism and Communism, and the fact that some of the chronic evils of mankind, notably wars, have in our day attained larger dimensions than at any earlier time and through implements which were first devised and multiplied in Christendom. On the other hand are great surges of life in Christianity which have made it as vigourous as at any time in its history and have planted it among more peoples than at any earlier time, so that it is more widely spread than it or any other religion has ever been.

This paradox is by no means new. It was seen spectacularly in the Cross, when the incarnation, life, and teachings of Christ were paralleled by his rejection and execution. It was prominent in the rise of Islam, which was in part provoked by Christianity and contained a distortion of the Gospel. It has been present throughout the centuries in Europe since the majority of the peoples of that continent became nominally Christian. In the Middle Ages at the very height of the great religious awakenings which gave rise, among other movements, to the Franciscans, Dominicans, Waldensees, and Cathari, and to the creative formulations of Christian faith which had the massive works of Thomas Aquinas as their peak, there were crass selfishness, callous cruelty, gross immorality, and ill-concealed and derisive scepticism, notably in the court of the Emperor Frederick II, the ranking monarch of the Europe of his day. The Renaissance and the secularistic humanism and the revival of much of the spirit of pagan antiquity which were associated with it were contemporary with such fresh commitments to the Gospel as Wycliffe, the Lollards, Hus, the Brethren of the Common Life, and some of the greatest of the German mystics. Machiavelli lived in the same generation as Luther. The moral degradation of the Papacy attained its most colossal dimensions within the hundred-year span which heard Savonarola preach repentance to the Florentines and which witnessed the beginnings of the Catholic and Protestant Reformations. At the very time that the "enlightenment" with its rationalism was undercutting zeal in many universities and among the intelligentsia, when the French Revolution was espousing Deism, when thousands were believing that Christianity was doomed, and when the wars of the French Revolution and Napoleon were shaking Europe to its foundations, the

173

Evangelical Awakening of which the Wesleys were outstanding leaders and the Great Awakening in the Thirteen Colonies followed by the Second Awakening and the revivals of the 1790's and the early 1800's were precursors of the forward surge of Christianity in the nineteenth century and were giving rise to the Sunday School and to missionary society after missionary society.

One is reminded of the parable (Matt. 13:24-30) where the householder declared that an enemy had sowed the tares among the good grain, but commanded that both wheat and tares be permitted to grow until the harvest. The imagery seems to say that both good and evil increase until the culmination of history, but that evil continues only with God's permission and that at the harvest it will be destroyed. There also comes to mind the passage in Revelation 12:12, where the devil is described as coming down "having great wrath, because he knoweth that he hath but a short time."

As one looks at recent and current trends he notes not only that our day is seeing the widest spread that the Gospel has ever known, the rooting of the Church in more peoples and cultures, and a more extensive influence of Christ upon mankind as a whole than at any earlier time, but also that this is increasingly through Protestantism. As we have seen, the Roman Catholic Church is vigourous and is growing rapidly in numbers in several countries, notably in Equatorial Africa, but proportionately Protestantism has been and is gaining more rapidly. Moreover, new movements of many kinds continue to issue from Protestantism, evidences of abounding vitality, and the impress of the Gospel upon mankind has latterly come much more through Protestantism than through

174

Roman Catholicism. Some of the examples from which this generalization is made are the Red Cross, Gandhi, the League of Nations, and the United Nations. In each of these, as we have pointed out, the influence of the Gospel was potent. That influence came through Protestantism and not through the Roman Catholic Church.

This might seem to indicate that the main stream of faith is henceforth to flow through Protestantism. Those of us who are Protestants are inclined to believe that this is because our branch of the faith is more nearly true to the Gospel than the Roman Catholic Church and very much more so than the Eastern Churches, for these appear to have lost the momentum which once made them missionary. We are tempted to hold that God's purpose in history will be finally accomplished through Protestantism.

However, we need to remember that Christ's Church is not identical with any one family of ecclesiastical institutions and that none of these fully expresses the mind of Christ. In each of them there are radiant, Christ-like souls in whom the fruits of the Spirit are seen. Nor is Protestantism as we know it God's final word. It, too, is under God's judgement, if for no other reason, because of its many competitive divisions and the tendency of these to group themselves by the social strata of the world in which they exist and thus to become class institutions. To a greater or less degree the paradox of which we have spoken is in each of the main organized branches of Christianity and in all the churches. The Church "which is the blessed company of all faithful people" is not identical with Protestantism or with any visible ecclesiastical structure.

Even individual Christians who undoubtedly show the fruits

175

of the Spirit are aware of the paradox within themselves. They are "being saved," to use Paul's apt expression. Paul himself, long after Christ had laid hold on him to make him his own, confessed that he had not attained and was not yet made perfect, and from him as a Christian came the poignant cry: "The good that I would I do not: but the evil which I would not, that do I. . . . O wretched man that I am! who shall deliver me from the body of this death?" And that was his experience, although immediately he breaks out in the triumphant and grateful shout: "I thank God through Jesus Christ our Lord."

Are these paradoxes ever to be resolved? Is the struggle to go on forever? Or is God ultimately to triumph? If He is to triumph, when and how will it be? Will it be within history or beyond history?

The confident Christian hope, based upon the promise of God who is faithful and "cannot deny Himself," is that it is His purpose to "gather together in one all things in Christ, both which are in heaven, and which are on earth." Inspired by God's Spirit Paul declared that "the creature was made subject to vanity" ("futility," or "meaninglessness" as other translations have it) "by reason of him who hath subjected the same in hope, because the creature" ("the creation," according to another translation) "itself also shall be delivered from the bondage of corruption into the glorious liberty of the children of God."

The victory has already been won by God who "having spoiled principalities and powers . . . made a shew of them openly, triumphing over them in him" (Christ), or in an alternative reading, "in it," namely, the Cross. The resurrection was a seal on that victory, for Jesus Christ "abolished death, and . . . brought life and immortality to light through the Gospel."

In Christ the "new age" began, the "age" to which the Hebrew prophets confidently looked forward. Christ not only proclaimed at the outset of his public ministry that the kingdom of God, where God's will is done, was "at hand," but later he declared that "the kingdom of God is come upon you" and that "the kingdom of God is among you" (or "is in the midst of you").

Yet it is clear that the kingdom of God is not yet fully come and that God's will is not now fully done. The reign of God is a present reality, but it is also a future hope. We are taught to pray: "Thy kingdom come, thy will be done on earth as it is in heaven," knowing that if the petition had been completely granted there would no longer be the need of offering it.

To what extent is God's kingdom already here? Where is God working? Where is His will being done, even if imperfectly? Here there is no agreement among Christians and convictions honestly differ. Some hold that "the prince of this world" is still in control in most of life, that what Augustine called "the earthly city" is wholly within his dominion and that God's salvation is operating only in the Church. Others declare that, while respecting men's wills, God is working in many, perhaps in all aspects of life—in business, in farming, in industry, in politics, in international relations, in science, in medicine, in music, in art, in education—although He obviously does not yet fully control them. They would point to the ways in which the influence of the Gospel is being seen. To some of these we have more than once called attention, as in the birth of the Red Cross, in the inception of the League of Nations and latterly of the United Nations, and in the life of

Gandhi. The evidence seems clearly to point in this direction.

Is God gradually, even though by uneven stages and with occasional temporary reverses, to transform human society within a continuation of the historical process as we have thus far known it? Will His will be fully done at some future stage of history? Many have believed and even now believe that this is to be. Especially under the influence of the conception of evolution which flourished late in the nineteenth century and in the optimism which was widespread in the Occident in the yesterday which came to a sudden twilight in 1914, this was a widely held conviction. In our day outside Christian circles there are non-Christian versions of this expectation. Such are Russian Communism, a secularistic "scientific" humanism, and some socialistic and democratic programs. Several features of the course of Christianity at which we have hinted appear to support this hope. Among them is that fact of which we have repeatedly spoken, that in spite of obstacles and the unprecedented magnitude of some of the hereditary evils of mankind Christianity is more widely spread, more deeply rooted among more peoples, and exerting a wider influence upon mankind than ever before.

However, against this expectation, what may be called this utopianism, are the testimony of history and the Scriptures. The paradoxes which we have noted seem to preclude such a culmination of history. At first sight the Scriptures appear to be ambiguous and to give ground both for the affirmation and the denial of the hope. Favouring it is the familiar commission to "make disciples of all nations, baptizing them . . . teaching them to observe" all that Christ commanded the inner group of his intimates. Surely, it may be argued, Christ would not have given that breath-taking injunction reinforced by the promise of his presence if he had not believed that it could and would be accomplished. So also Paul declared that God consigned all to disobedience that He might have mercy on all and, as we have more than once noted, John's Gospel says that "God sent not his Son into the world to condemn the world; but that the world through him might be saved." Yet other passages clearly preclude the hope of the full attainment of this purpose within history. Christ spoke of the gate and the road which lead to destruction. In his famous picture of the last judgement he described some as going away into everlasting punishment and some into life eternal. In the parable of the wheat and the tares there is the eventual decisive separation of the two. Again and again in the New Testament the changes are rung on this theme and in varied imagery.

The New Testament is emphatic that there is to be an end of history. The Bible is clear that history had a beginning and is to have a culmination and that both are the act of God. The precise details of that culmination are not given us. We are warned not to attempt to discover the time when it will be and yet to live as though it might come at the next moment. Since it is without precedent in history we cannot compare it or parallel it with anything of which history tells us. In the Bible figures of speech are necessarily employed to describe it. The frequent attempts which have been made to forecast the shape and date of the end of history have often been dogmatic but they have done violence to the purpose of the Scriptures. We should have been warned away from them by the words of the risen Christ. When the disciples, stirred to a joyous hope by the resurrection, asked whether he was at that time to restore the kingdom to Israel, which, in spite of their long association with him was the only form in which they could conceive of the climax of history, Christ told them that it was not for them to know the times or the seasons, but expressed his quiet conviction that "the Father hath put [them] in his own power," thus reminding them both that God is the lord of history and that we cannot always know His ways. For us the precise manner and hour of the culmination of history must remain a mystery.

Yet, while living in instant expectation of that event we are not to be disappointed if it is greatly delayed. Like the wise virgins in the parable, we are to be prepared for what may seem the tardy coming of the bridegroom. It was the foolish virgins who were so sure of his early arrival that they made what proved to be insufficient provision.

In the meantime we are not to be idle. We are to be witnesses. As servants we are to go about the duties assigned to us as though our Master might appear at any moment. In the intricacies of the many relations which in our day bind us in the same bundle with all mankind, we must endeavour even now to live as members of God's kingdom. We must labour to permeate all features of human society with the teachings of Christ. We must aim at nothing less than winning all the nations to discipleship, incorporating them in Christ's Church, and teaching them to bring all aspects of their life into conformity with Christ's commands.

Even though we know that, by a paradox, the goal is not to be attained within history, we must press forward toward it. Although the apostle was clear-eyed about the Christians to whom he ministered, with their weaknesses and imperfections he prayed that they might know the love of Christ, although he declared that it passes knowledge, and be filled unto all the fullness of God. In this he was but following his Master who commanded his disciples to be perfect as their Father in heaven is perfect. Part of the wonder of the Gospel is that it inspires us to reach toward perfection, knowing that God has commanded us to do so, that the command is in love, and that His love will not fail us. He does not call us to the seemingly unattainable in such a way as to leave us frustrated, breathlessly striving to bring ourselves and all men to a standard which always eludes us, moving on before us like a will-o'-the-wisp or the end of a rainbow. If the goal were one which could be gained we would either be smug and self-satisfied when we had attained it or else restless that there was nothing more to work for. Before us is always the beckoning challenge of the impossible for ourselves as individuals and collectively for the Church and mankind as a whole. Yet along the way there is a growing depth of humble appreciation of the love of God in Christ, an increasing knowledge of God Who is love, and a deepening and ever-enriching fellowship with Him and with others of His children. There is the assurance that these will continue after history has come to an end. The God and Father of our Lord Jesus Christ is lord of the past, the present, and the future in all the vast universe which He has created and which He sustains. In Christ we see His purpose for that universe, for the human race, and for every one of the untold billions of individuals who comprise and have comprised mankind. In what manner, precisely by what steps, and when He is to consummate that purpose we cannot know. We can, however, seek to rise to the privilege of being co-workers with Him and to share in the fulfilment of the world mission of the Church in this day which we call ours but which is His gift. We can do so, knowing, not merely wistfully hoping, that neither things present nor things to come can separate us from the love of God which is in Christ Jesus our lord.

181

Index

Adams, John Quincy, 145
Afghanistan, 7
Africa, revolution in, 19, 65; in the nineteenth century, 48–49; race tensions in, 61, 148, 152; restlessness of masses in, 63, 103; Roman Catholic indigenous clergy in, 88; after 1914, 102–107, 131; *see also* South Africa
Agnosticism, 23, 72
America, Latin. *See* Latin America
American Board of Commissioners for Foreign Missions, 33, 41
American Friends Service Committee, 97–98
Americas, Christianity in, 43–47; social and economic revolution in, 66–67; *see also various countries*
Andover Theological Seminary, 41
Anglo-Catholics, 34–35
Angola, 103
Animism, 56, 72, 105, 125
Anti-clericalism, 24, 26, 47
Aquinas, Thomas, 173
Arabia, 108
Arabs, 61, 107
Argentina, 99
Armaments production, 61
Armenians, 107
Ashram, 112
Asia. *See various countries*
Augustine, 177
Australasia, social and economic revolutions in, 66
Australia, 18, 43, 47, 100
Austria, 16, 66

Awakening, Great, 30, 174; Evangelical, 30, 174; Second Great, 30, 174

Bantu, 104–105, 148
Baptists, in Russia, 42, 80; in the United States, 93, 95; in Canada, 98; in Burma, 115
Bataks, 101, 169
Belgian Congo, 103, 104, 107
Berdyaev, 78
Berlin, 75
Bethlehem, 149
Bible, historical study of, 22–23; translations of, 49, 166
Bible societies, 33
Boer War, 16
Brahmo Samaj, 51, 58
"Brain-washing," 119
Brazil, 47, 99, 100
"Brethren," 139
Brethren of the Common Life, 173
British Guiana, 29
Buddhism, 51, 52, 56, 72, 73, 77, 113, 115, 117, 125
Bulgaria, 24
Burma, in British Empire, 18; nineteenth-century, 51–52; independence of, 63, 114; since 1914, 113–115

Canada, 43, 98; United Church of, 84
Carey, William, 146
Caste structure, Indian, 109
Catholic Action, 25

INDEX

in, 63; condition of Christianity in, today, 75–77; Protestant unity in, 82; contrasted with United States, 90, 97; missionary activity in, 97; *see also various countries*

"Evangelical," 33

Evangelical Alliance, 33

Evangelical Awakening, 30, 174

Evangelical Church, in Germany, 82

Evangelical and Reformed Church, in United States, 84

Evangelicals, in Russia, 42, 80

Evangelism, 163–166

Evolution theory, 17–18, 23, 178

Exploitation, missionary criticism of, 38; industrial revolution and, 143; of African masses, 148

Faith and Order, World Conference on, 82

Family of Jesus, 123

Fascists, 79

Federal Council of the Churches of Christ in America, 33

Fellowship, world-wide, 8, 132

Finney, Charles G., 31

Food supply, improved, 38, 55

Formosa, 119

France, empire of, 18; de-Christianization in, 24, 75, 78–79; Revolution in, 22, 25, 173; monastic orders in, 25; Protestant revival in, 31; McCall Mission in, 42; in Indo-China, 62, 63, 115; Roman Catholicism in, 79; Reformed Church unified in, 82

Franco-Prussian War, 16

Frederick II, 173

Free Church of Scotland, 43

Free thought, 22

Free will, 151, 153

French Canadians, 98

Frontier, United States, 45, 89, 90

Gandhi, 62, 108–109, 110–111, 133, 175, 178

Germany, Protestantism in, 28–29, 30, 31, 42, 75; Pietism in, 31; Inner Mission in, 42; revolution in, 66; inflation in, 70; since 1914, 75; Nazis in, 78, 148; Roman Catholicism in, 79; East, Christianity in, 80; Evangelical Church in, 82

God, judgement of, 140–150, 175, 179; as love, 140, 171, 181; ideal of, for men, 140, 141; power and love of, 171; kingdom of, 177–178

Gold Coast, 104, 163

Gospel, power of, 7, 45, 87–88, 101; enemies of, 8, 71–75, 86; nature of, 10; influence of, in Western civilization, 20, 45–46; moral and spiritual effect of, 36, 49, 50, 51, 58; spread of, 36–59, 86–136; preparation for, 40; deeper understanding of, 77; universality of, 88; perversion of, 105, 141, 172; continued potency of, 137–150; urgency of proclamation of, 152; and evangelism, 163–166; personal commitment to, 164; inspiration of, 181; *see also* Christianity

Great Awakening, 30, 174

Great Britain, empire of, 18; established church in, 29; Evangelical Awakening in, 30; Protestant revival in, 30, 31; separation of church and state in, 32; missionary societies in, 41; Roman Catholic Church in, 42; achievements in, of missionary enterprise, 42–43; revolution in, 66; decline of Christianity in, 75; union of churches in, 81; Council of Churches in, 82; slavery abolished in, 146; *see also* Church of England

185

187

Maoris, 16
Mar Thoma Church, 51, 109
Maritain, Jacques, 79
Mark, Gospel of, 137
Marx, Karl, 17, 23, 67, 143–144
Mass society, 73–74, 75, 77, 78, 93, 153
Matthew, Gospel of, 174
Medicine, Western, 49, 50, 54, 70, 133; schools for training in, 38–39, 58, 110; reappraisal of mission-supported medical institutions, 160
Mela, 112
Methodism, 30, 81; in Korea, 56; in United States, 84, 93, 95
Mexico, 47, 98–99, 100
Ministry, increase in numbers ordained in, 96; preparation for, 162
Mission and unity, 153–154
Missionaries, Pietist, 30; coöperation of, 34; protection of, by home governments, 37; achievements of, in nineteenth century, 37–39, 41–59, 87; criticism of exploitation voiced by, 38; factors in appraising work of, before 1914, 57–59; after 1914, 97–131, 133–135; decline in staffs of, 134–135; all Christians as, 153, 155; reëxamination of enterprises of, 156–161; occupation of, with administration, 161; recruiting, preparation, and attitudes of, 166–169; from "younger churches," 169; *see also* Protestantism *and* Roman Catholic Church
Missionary societies, 33–34, 40–41, 155, 174
Mobility, loss of, among missionaries, 134–135; regaining of, 157, 162–163; and evangelism, 163

Modern mass society, 73–74, 75, 77, 78, 93, 153
Modernism, 25
Mohammed, 76
Monastic orders, 25, 173
Money, lower purchasing power of, 70
Mongolia, Outer, 7–8
Monks as early missionaries, 40
Moody, Dwight L., 31, 41, 147
Moravians, 30, 40
Morley-Minto reforms, 62
Moros, 55
Morrison, Robert, 146–147
Moslems, 20, 40, 49, 52, 55; after 1914, 107–108

Napoleonic Wars, 15, 25, 173
National Christian Council of China, 120
National Christian Council of India, Burma, and Ceylon, 111
National Christian Council of Japan, 128, 129
National Council of the Churches of Christ in the United States of America, 84
Nationalism, 72, 73, 102, 113, 114, 115, 118, 143, 160
Nationalist Government in China, 117, 119
Natural resources, Russian, 67; United States, 68; Brazilian, 99; African, 102–103
Nazis, 79, 148
Near East Christian Council, 108
Negroes, abolition of slavery of, 20, 31, 45, 146; Christianity among, in United States, 45, 90, 92; education of, 93; northward migration of, 94
Nehru, Motilal, 73
Nepal, 7
Nestorian Church, 107
Netherlands, 31, 62
New Guinea, 101

New Hebrides, 101
New Zealand, 16, 18, 43, 100
Nietzsche, 22
Nigeria, 104
Nonconformist churches, 31, 82
Norwegian Lutheran Church of America, 84
Nursing, 31, 39, 58, 133

Occident. *See* Western civilization
Okinawa, 169
Opium wars, 145
Optimism, 15, 17–18, 178
Orthodox Churches, in nineteenth century, 24; in Japan, 42, 57, 88; in United States, 77, 84, 92; since 1914, 77–78, 86, 128; *see also* Greek Orthodox Church *and* Russian Orthodox Church
Oxford Movement, 34

Pacific islands, 19, 47–48, 100–101
Pakistan, 62, 73, 108, 112, 113
Paris, 78
Passing of the Great Race, The, 63
Paul, 138–139, 141, 149, 176, 179
Pax Britannica, 114
Peace, in nineteenth century, 15, 16, 60; efforts to promote, 20, 32
Pentecost, 139
People's Republic of China, 119
Pessimism, 63
Philippines, 55, 116, 131, 169
Pietism, 30, 31
Pius X, 27
Plymouth Brethren, 32
Poland, revolution in, 66; Communism in, 79; Y.M.C.A. in, 82
Polish National Catholic Church, 84
Polynesia, 47–48, 100–101
Polytheism, 72, 125
Popes, 24–25; power of, 26–27; moral degradation of, 173
Populations, migrations of, 18, 23 (*see also* Immigration); increase

and pressure of, 70, 108, 113, 152; migrations of, within United States, 94
Portugal, 76
Positivism, 47
Poverty, in Western Europe, 61, 97, 134
Presbyterians, in Scotland, 31; in Korea, 56, 127; in United States, 96; in Canada, 98
Prices, rising, 70
Priesthood, indigenous, 88, 106, 109, 120, 132; of all believers, 151
Prison reform, 20, 31
Propaganda, Communist, 64, 67; of democracy, 68; Japanese, 130
Progress, belief in, 17
"Prophets," African, 105
Protestantism, in nineteenth century, 27–35, 41–59; divisions in, 28, 32, 175; principles of, 28, 31, 151; regionalism in, 28, 29; in Germany, 28–29, 30, 31, 42, 75; movement toward unity in, 29, 32–35, 81–85, 100, 111–112, 113, 129; in the United States, before 1914, 29, 30, 31, 43–46; revivals of, 30–34, 80–85; reforms spurred by, 31–32, 45–46, 175; early missionaries of, 37, 38, 39, 40; in Scandinavia, 42; in Japan, 42, 57, 128, 129, 130–131; in France, 42; in Russia, 42, 80; in Great Britain, 42–43; in Latin America, 47, 100; among the Polynesians, 48; in Africa, 48–49, 103–105, 106, 107; in India, 49–50, 109, 111; in Ceylon, 51, 113; in Burma and Thailand, 52; in China, in nineteenth century, 54–55; in the Philippines, 55, 116; in Korea, 56, 127; since 1914, 80–85, 86, 92–132, 135; in United States, after 1914, 86, 92–97; adminis-

191